Sincerely,

Addison's Sister

a memoir

Sincerely,

Addison's Sister

a memoir

jessica sharp akhrass

Copyright © 2019 Jessica Akhrass. All rights reserved. No part of this book may be used or reproduced in any form without express written permission from the author and/or publisher except for brief quotes, approved excerpts, articles, and reviews.

For information, quotes, excerpts, interview requests, speaking engagement bookings, and group order discounts, contact the author or publisher.

jessica_akhrass@yahoo.com
Facebook: A.D.D.I.S.O.N.

Crippled Beagle Publishing
Knoxville, Tennessee
dyer.cbpublishing@gmail.com

Cover design by Lauren Hartness

Paperback ISBNS 978-1970037319, 978-1970037357
Hardcover ISBN 978-1970037326

Library of Congress Control Number: 2020903646

In a contemporary memoir, stories are told as the author can best recall. Dialogue, event details, and descriptions are as accurate as possible given the frailties of the human memory and the trauma experienced by the author.

Printed in the United States of America

For My Parents,

Who taught me how to love, the meaning of hard work,

Who exhibited the example of married life that most aspire to have,

And introduced us to a life with Christ.

Special thanks to my loving husband,

Who supported my mission and calling every step of the way,

Who held me up and many times carried me,

And loved me through it all, even when I was at my most unlovable.

Special thanks to Susie Slyman,

Who has loved me and stood beside me through the absolute best,

And absolute worst of times.

Who is one that I know will always be there,

As my mother, mentor, and friend.

We love you, Gigi.

Special thanks to Sandy Jones,

Who answered her calling and came to walk beside me,

Who loved me, encouraged me, and prayed me through this entire journey.

We love you, Oma.

Special thanks to Vickie McGee Bellamy,

My Godmother and my mother's best friend since fourth grade,

Who has given wise advice on my political journey,

And who is, has always been, and will always be there when I need her.

We love you, Tutu.

Special thanks to Wanda Carder,

Who moved into our neighborhood before Addison was even born,

But became fast friends with my parents,

And has remained part of our family to this day, always providing love and support.

We love you, Nana.

To Addison's Facebook Family,

Who rallied with me in our grass roots campaign,

Who rooted, cheered, and prayed me onward.

Who wrote letters and emails and made all the phone calls needed,

You made our mission a success.

WE did this, together.

In loving memory of Jeffery Addison Sharp,

My baby brother who held my heart in the palm of his hand from day one.

You are never far from my mind or my heart.

I carry you with me every day,

and know that every year that passes without you

Is another year that I am closer to seeing your sweet face again.

I love you.

October 24, 1989 – January 2, 2012

the window

BAM!!! I recognized the sound before I even had a chance to open my eyes. It was a little after one in the morning and though I had just barely drifted off. I assume that the sound of shattering glass would have woken me from a dead sleep. The room was dark except for the light from the flat screen television that hung on the wall across from our bed. God, that thing was a bitch to hang. The TV is always on at night; I can't sleep without it. More times than not my husband Sam will make a subtle attempt to retrieve the remote from my clenched hand and turn it off on the rare occasion that I doze off before he does, but, unfortunately for both of us, the click of the television and the silence in the room that follows immediately rouses me. He always complains that the noise and the light keep him awake, but I witness him night after night fall fast into slumber the minute his head meets the pillow. It takes me much longer. I can't turn my mind off. I have to work my way into sleep. My favorite things to sleep to are real life crime shows *Dateline, American Justice*, and *48 Hours Mystery*. Sam can't understand how I can fall asleep listening to accounts of heinous rapes, kidnappings, and murders, but that's just the point. I listen. Aside from the fact that forensic science has always fascinated me, I don't have to actually watch those shows. The narrators tell the story and for whatever reason, this narration quiets my brain. It keeps me focused on one thing while I close my eyes and wait for sleep, hoping that I will dream of him again. It was September of 2012, and Sam, a dentist, was out of the country on a mission trip, providing free dental care to the citizens of a town in Trinidad. I don't like being in the house alone all night. What little comfort I have comes from my dogs, especially Ellie, the Great Pyrenees. I suspect that dog would die trying to protect me if she had to. She guards us, and she guards the house. That's what I say to her when I am leaving, "Ellie, you're in charge. Guard the house," and she does. We had lived in our house for eight years, in quiet Lenoir City, Tennessee, just nine miles from the house that I grew up in with my parents in neighboring Knoxville. The crime rate is low and I had always felt safe here but not that night.

BAM!!! Someone broke the window in our master bathroom. I practically fell out of the bed. I'd like to say that I sprang covertly, with stealth catlike precision to reach for my 20 gauge shotgun, which I kept loaded and lying under my bed. I basically kangarooed myself onto the floor and in an instant half-blindly blew a hole the size of a saucer through my bathroom door.

All three dogs had been sleeping like one hundred-pound gremlin pods in the bed with me. Instead of jumping to my defense, they tucked their tails and disappeared to hide in the living room. I couldn't blame them, and I couldn't believe what was happening. Someone or maybe a group was out there. I assumed they were gone by this point, especially after my shotgun blast. Still, someone was in my backyard. Someone was inside my fence in the middle of the night. Sam was gone, and I was all alone. Pacing, and trembling, I struggled with the decision of whom to call. *Not the police*, I thought. I didn't want to call them. What if somehow this ended up on the news? That was the last thing I wanted. It seemed like every time I turned on the news in those days, there I was. I had previously welcomed the media exposure, but I didn't want this story out. Whoever was out there was at the very least trying to frighten me, and they had, but I wasn't about to publicly admit that.

With everything that my family had recently endured, I couldn't bear to startle them with a middle-of-the-night phone call. I figured the one person close by who would be awake at that hour was my best friend Amanda. Following my frantic phone call, Amanda sent her husband Paul (with his handgun in tow) on his way to my house while I surveyed the damage I had done to the bathroom. The hole I blew through the bathroom door was impressive. What was more impressive was my aim. Even though I was born and raised in the rolling hills of East Tennessee, I wasn't good with guns. In fact, they terrify me, but I managed to hit the bathroom door in the vicinity where the sound of the breaking glass had originated without hitting the television or killing any of my dogs, and I did so without the kickback from the shotgun knocking my one-hundred-pound frame to the floor. I slowly crept around the now splintered door to flip the light switch and illuminate the dark bathroom. A jumble of belts that had been hanging on a shoe rack on the opposite side of the door were blown completely off and onto the linoleum. Buckshot littered the floor. I stood there, mouth agape, and stared at the bowling ball sized whole in the large bay window above the jacuzzi tub. Though I should have expected it, my body still jolted when I heard a knock at the door. It was Paul.

He snickered at me with the little laugh that practically drives Amanda to insanity. "Oh my God," he said. "I can't believe you shot a hole through the door. Oh, my, God," he continued chuckling.

"Okay, Paul! What was I supposed to do? Wait until they climbed all the way into the damn bathroom?" I responded. He sounded like a kid on Christmas morning, giddy, as he stared at the damage and giggled some more. "This is serious, Paul! Someone was in the backyard. Did you bring your gun?" I asked.

"Yep!" He reached around and pulled the semi-automatic handgun from the back of the waistband of his camouflage green cargo shorts. He eyed his gun, seemingly happy to have it out for real protection rather than just target practice at the range.

"Let's go look around outside," I said, "I'm sure they're gone, but I won't be able to sleep until we look. And be careful with that gun. The only thing worse than this being on the news is if the headline is, 'Best friend's Husband Shoots Himself in the Foot While Looking for Intruder.'"

We were quiet as we headed out the front door and into the darkness. It was a clear, slightly cool night in early fall, my favorite time of the year. The leaves on the plentiful trees had not yet changed, nor had Daylight Savings Time ended, and everyone was enjoying the respite from yet another hot, humid, Southern summer. My heart pounded as we crept around to the back of the house. I followed Paul closely, walking in a quieted crouch, one hand entwined in a death grip with the back of his T-shirt. "Why do I feel like WE are the criminals?" I whispered.

"We aren't. We're like snipers," he whispered back.

He was a child playing army, and I tried not to giggle as I responded, "Well, don't step in a big pile of dog shit with those flip flops on, G.I. Joe."

A six-foot, planked wooden fence that my husband and I constructed with the help of my dad and my grandfather cordons off our gently sloped backyard. Each of the three sides of the enclosure has an oversized gate. We entered the backyard through the gate on the left side of the house, Paul was in front holding up his trusty handgun, and I followed closely behind with a flashlight shining over his left shoulder. We approached the broken window with caution, examining the ground in search of a hammer, a brick, a rock, or whatever was used to smash the glass. Curiously, we found nothing, proving, I guess, that not all criminals are stupid. Empty-handed, we headed toward the opposite oversized gate on the right side of the yard, which is where the criminals had obviously escaped. The gate stood partially open about two feet. We sneaked through to the other side and tiptoed down along the fence line until we had covered the entire perimeter of the yard. It was quiet except for the crickets and spring peeper frogs from the woods beyond our property. It was obvious that whoever was there was long gone by now. We both breathed a sigh of relief, and I untangled my fingers from his T-shirt as Paul lowered his gun and asked, "Wanna smoke?"

Feeling much more at ease, Paul and I perched ourselves on the back deck and enjoyed our cigarettes. I let the dogs out into the backyard with us and as they were busily nosing around in the grass, Paul and I discussed the situation.

"That window sits so high off the ground," Paul said. "I wonder how they thought they were going to get in?"

"Maybe they weren't planning on coming in," I replied. "I don't think they were thieves. I think they did exactly what they came to do—scare the shit out of me. How did they even know where I live? We're unlisted. I got those threatening emails a while back, but I didn't actually think someone would come to my house."

"People can find out anything nowadays, and you've been on the news so many times, people could find out somehow," Paul said. "Plus, you've pissed a lot of people off with this whole thing. Maybe you should reconsider and back off, you know, just let it go."

"No way!" I snapped indignantly, "People are dying, Paul, and I've come too far. I can't stop now."

room one

"Call Addison," she said. I knew immediately that something was wrong. I could always tell by her inflection and tone when my mother was worried. "I just called his phone and his speech sounded slurred; call him from your phone and see if you think he sounds strange" she said. My stomach dropped because I knew before I even called him that he wouldn't sound right. After the morning I had spent with him that very same day and all that I had witnessed, I expected him to sound slurred. I didn't, however, expect him to ignore my phone calls.

Every call went to voicemail. My socked feet paced the bedroom floor, practically wearing a hole in the carpet as I waited for an answer. When multiple attempts failed, I knew that my only option was to call his roommate, his roommate whom I hated, his roommate who slithered into Addison's life, his roommate who lived in an apartment that my parents paid for, his roommate who didn't ask my parents' permission and never offered any contribution toward paying the bills, his roommate—the drug addict.

I will never call Addison's roommate his "friend," though that is what they called each other. Addison met the guy at his very first job during the summer after he graduated from high school. He was no friend. To me, he was a leech, a street urchin, mooching off every ounce of kindness anyone offered him and sucking them dry. He was a user of anyone kind enough to give him a handout. Without batting an eye, he lied, cheated, and stole from his "friends." I held my breath as I called his roommate several times before he actually answered.

Angrily, and without introduction I asked, "WHERE is my brother?"

"I don't know, man. I'm in the living room playing Xbox," he replied in his typical detached nonchalant murmur which always frustrated me.

"Well, can you get up off your ASS and go LOOK? He was JUST talking to my mother not ten minutes ago, and now I can't get him to answer the phone, so what the hell is going on over there!?!" I yelled. Without responding, his roommate began fumbling through the two-bedroom apartment that they shared. There was an anxious churning in my gut. I knew something was terribly wrong as I realized that my only connection and communication to discovering how serious the situation was lay in the hands of a complete idiot.

"Well, um, okay," he hesitantly stammered.

"WHAT? What is it?" I pleaded.

"Okay, so, like, Addison is in his bathroom, and . . . ."

"AND WHAT? What? What's WRONG?" I interrupted.

"So, he's in the bathroom, and he's sort of, like, halfway in the tub, but then sort of, like, halfway out," he apathetically explained. More disturbing than what his roommate was telling me was that I heard him giggle while describing my brother's limp body, passed out on the bathroom floor. He smirked. I could actually *hear* the little bastard snicker. Somehow, he thought this was funny?? I was terrified. Trembling, heart pounding, knees quaking, terrified.

"Could you check and see if Addison is DEAD? Does he have a pulse?" I don't know why I was still surprised that his roommate didn't bother to check to see if my brother was alive.

He simply stated, "Nah man, he's okay. He does this, like, all the time. He's just asleep. He'll just sleep really good for a while, and then he'll wake up and he'll be fine. It's cool."

"It's COOL? IT'S COOL!?!" I bellowed. Is this kid for REAL? Immediately, my accusations began, "What did he take? What did YOU give him?" It truly is like pulling teeth to get the truth out of an addict. Precious minutes were being wasted as I was arguing with this imbecile who kept repeating, "I don't know, man! Don't blame me. I don't watch him every second! I don't know what he took!" In what seemed like an eternity, I eventually got what I was sure was a partial truth, "I mean, he probably took like six or eight Xanax bars, maybe, but trust me, it's fine, he does this like every other day." But it wasn't fine. My brother wasn't FINE. Addison was unconscious at best. That is what I immediately began praying for: that Addison was just unconscious and not something incredibly worse.

The phone barely had a chance to fully ring one time before I heard my mother's voice, "Well, what did he sound like to you?"

"I didn't get to talk to him," I said as I stumbled out of my pajama pants, frantically searching for my jeans. "He's taken some pills, he's passed out on the bathroom floor, do you want me to call an ambulance?" Though muffled, I could hear my mother lurch from her bed, scrambling as she smacked my dad's arm, "Get UP! Addison's passed out on the floor!"

"What do you want me to do, Mom?" I cried.

"Meet us at Baptist," she said, "I'll call Orbin."

As we hung up I yelled for Sam, who was busily working on something in his office. "It's Addison!" I screamed in a panic. Adrenaline pulsed through my veins as frenzied prayers flew out of my mouth. "PLEASE let him be okay," I prayed. "Please, God don't let him die; what if he dies? What will we do? Oh God, please help me, please let us get there fast enough!"

Half-dressed, my mother called my grandfather Orbin as she raced for the back door. Technically, Orbin is not my grandfather but rather my step-grandfather, having married my maternal grandmother when I was about five years old, but we never used the word "step." Orbin is a retired Marine and the toughest, yet one of the sweetest, men I've ever known. He is not a blood relative, but he is my grandfather, nonetheless. I was merely acquainted with my biological grandfather and saw him only annually for an uncomfortable visit with a man I barely knew. The only things I ever heard about him were unpleasant, and from my experiences, he was nothing like Orbin. Orbin would do anything for any of us, and I loved him immediately. He is one of my best friends. When any one of us ever needed anything, especially in a pinch, we called Orbin.

Raindrops the size of golf balls pounded the windshield of our Honda S2000 with a deafening sound and the fierce wind was howling on that freezing January night. I watched the red-orange glow from our digital speedometer climb to 80, then 90 and beyond as Sam feverishly drove while I rocked myself back and forth in the passenger seat. We didn't speak. Sam was concentrating, and I was trying my best to self-soothe. I couldn't cry. I was hysterical, and my hands and feet were sweating, but there were no tears. My prayers were on repeat, "Please let him be okay. Please don't let him die."

I can only visualize the scene at Addison's apartment when my parents arrived. I'm unsure if his roommate stuck around until they got there, or if he took off for fear of punishment because he knew that his involvement with Addison's condition was substantial. After bursting through the unlocked apartment door, they headed straight for the bathroom where they found Addison just as the roommate had described: on the floor and unconscious. Without pause, Orbin flipped Addison's motionless body over his shoulder like a 175-pound sack of potatoes. He carried him down the dark, narrow stairway from the apartment, out into the driving rain and placed him in the backseat of my parents' car.

My family was already in the waiting area when Sam and I burst into the emergency room. I hate hospitals, as many people do. The sterile smell, the fluorescent lighting, and the coldness of the walls and floors have always sent a noticeably uncomfortable feeling through my body. The ever-present adrenaline rush was forcing me to pace back and forth across the recently mopped, yet still germ-riddled floor. *I want to see him. What is taking so long?!* I gained a slight reprieve when I was told that was Addison was awake. *Thank you GOD. He is awake.* My prayers had been answered. Addison was alive. Addison was awake; however, Addison was angry.

We felt helpless. Having just turned nineteen the previous October, Addison was no longer a minor, and he exercised his adult rights by not allowing my parents admittance into his hospital room. My parents were forced into the waiting area with Orbin, Sam, and me despite my mother's desperate plea, "I don't care how old he is! He's my CHILD!" Sam tried his best to calm and comfort my family, but there was nothing else we could do but wait. We were the only souls in the emergency room that night. It was cold, the storm outside had not subsided, and the air was thick with fear. Few words were spoken between us. We didn't know what to say.

About 30 minutes into our wait, I couldn't take it anymore. No one was telling us anything. No updates, no reports, nothing. I found a nurse and begged her to go ask Addison to let me into his room. I was elated when she returned through the two oversized automatic doors leading into the emergency room and motioned for me to follow her. As I approached Room 1, the door was partially open and I could see Addison. He was groggy, hooked to an IV, and his beautiful, big brown eyes were bloodshot, fire engine red. I was so happy and relieved to see him awake and looking at me. I tried not to let the tears spill, and as I approached him I could see the rage on his face began to bubble up to the surface. "I HATE YOU, JESSICA! I FUCKING HATE YOU!" Slouched in his hospital bed, he hissed hateful words and glared at me through squinted, infuriated eyes.

He hated me for calling our parents. He hated me for bringing to everyone's attention something that we had suspected for some time now. He hated me for *knowing*, and for letting the whole family know with certainty, that he was using drugs. I knew he didn't mean it. We loved each other. We fought hard and often said things we didn't mean, like most siblings, but we loved hard, too. Suddenly a nurse was in my face and pushing me back out of the room. I yelled back at my brother, "I don't care if you hate me Addison. You can hate me forever! Just as long as you're alive, you can hate me forever!" I honestly don't remember if I told him I loved him during that exchange. I would like to think that I did. It wouldn't have mattered anyway; he KNEW that I loved him.

A few hours later, we were able to take Addison home to my parents' house. We left the hospital still knowing very little about what Addison's condition actually was or what doctors had done to treat him. He was an adult, they kept reminding us, and he hadn't given his consent for us to know. Addison and I rode together in Orbin's car. He acted as though he didn't remember screaming at me and saying he hated my guts. He could barely hold his head up as we drove home in the middle of the night. His speech was slurred, and his eyes were at half-mast. Between his index and middle finger, he held a lit cigarette as it burned down to the filter because he forgot to smoke it. Seeing my brother in that condition was horrible. I hurt from the inside out. I was heartbroken.

Once home from the hospital, Addison slept three solid days. Orbin stayed on watch in case Addison awoke and tried to sneak out while my parents and I researched online for rehab facilities. We eventually chose a Christian-based, all-boys treatment center, which used, among other things, canine therapy, and was located in the middle of nowhere in Arkansas. The next morning, we were cautiously hopeful as we boarded a private airplane owned by one of my father's longtime friends to take my brother to Capstone Treatment Facility. Of course, we were apprehensive about leaving him there. He would stay four months. But he had agreed to go, and we were somewhat relieved. At that moment, we had hope and never suspected that that terrible night of January 6 would not be our last trip to Room 1.

orientation

The terrifying night of Addison's Xanax overdose should not have surprised me. From what I had experienced earlier that same morning, I should have seen it coming.

In January of 2009, Addison was about to begin his first semester at The University of Tennessee, which is a large university located on a sprawling campus that is attended by roughly 30,000 students each year. I didn't mind escorting my little brother to orientation. After all, compared to the small private Catholic high school that Addison had attended, The University of Tennessee (UT) could appear very intimidating. Having graduated from UT seven years earlier, I knew the campus very well.

You would have to know my brother to understand that his request for a wake-up call at the ungodly hour of 6:30 a.m. was expected. Addison did not yet understand the concept of any human being rising before the sun and thus far had proved to be completely incapable of accomplishing that feat on his own. Being the good sister that I was, I began calling him at 6:15 that morning. Naturally, there was no answer, which also did not surprise me. The prior year I had purchased him something called the "Sonic Boom Alarm Clock" in the hopes that it would blast him out of the bed when he needed to wake, but that too apparently had failed, assuming that Addison had remembered to plug it in.

I repeatedly called my brother again and again while driving to pick up our dad, who was accompanying us to orientation. I wish that I could remember why we both were taking him, but unfortunately I cannot. The only reasonable explanation is that Addison was not trusted with my father's credit card any longer, which was a wise decision, and Addison needed it during student orientation. I continued to call Addison to no avail along the ten-minute drive from my parents' house to Addison's apartment. I grew evermore frustrated with each unanswered call.

After bounding, two steps at a time, up the narrow staircase to the second-floor apartments, I feverishly pounded on Addison's front door. After the second, or maybe it was the third BANG, BANG, BANG with my fist, the door to the dark apartment finally opened. What I saw in the shadows of the open doorway was shocking. In a stupor and leaning into the doorframe was a frail and sedated Addison, fully dressed in jeans and a short-sleeved, purple polo shirt, which was his favorite color. He was disheveled and feeble looking, and it quickly became obvious that my little brother was drugged. He was unable to stand on his own, and his neck was incapable of holding up his drooping head.

I said nothing when I saw him; I assume I was in shock. Without saying a word, he turned from me and shuffled toward his bedroom in the back of the apartment. I followed slowly, examining the chaotic mess in the living room that my brother had produced along with the three or four friends whose passed out bodies I was now stepping over as I crossed the apartment floor. The apartment was dingy, and the smell of stale cigarette and pot smoke lingered in the air. A giant *Scarface* poster hung on the wall behind the couch.

Ashtrays covered tables while tiny cigarette-sized burn marks appeared to aerate the carpet, empty beer cans were scattered everywhere, and a giant silver hookah pipe lay on the main living room table.

Addison made it to his bedroom door, not on his own accord, but by bouncing off every available wall space along the way. He had slept in his wrinkled clothes, which he normally might do on purpose to save precious last moments of sleep, but I quickly realized that his had not been a well-laid plan, but instead the scenario and his state were consequences of the night before. I followed my brother as he stumbled his way into the bathroom, and I tried to make sense of what was happening.

My breath caught in my throat in horror as I watched my brother prop himself against the bathroom counter with one hand and attempt to brush his teeth, in vain, with the other. Dropping his toothbrush, he lethargically spit into the sink. Then he leaned down in front of me and slurred, "Will you . . . brush my hair?" He couldn't look at me as he struggled to keep his beautiful yet listless eyes open. Addison had puppy dog eyes of deep dark brown with eyelashes that any woman would envy. They were nearly an inch long on the top and as black as night. I did pick up the brush and comb his hair lightly while my mind raced, *What IS this? What drug is he on? Is this HEROIN?* I had no idea. It never entered my mind that Addison took prescription pills. I knew the substance was something awful, but I had no idea what was happening.

I was trapped between complete fright and anger. I was angry with him for taking any drug and even angrier that I didn't know what drug it was or what other negative consequences may lie ahead. I was terrified. This wasn't my baby brother Addison, the cherub-faced little boy I loved from the time I could see his little foot poking and his body rolling against the inside of my mother's growing belly. This wasn't the little boy who could make anyone laugh at any moment, the boy at whom no one could ever stay angry. This was frightening. He was someone else, someone barely able to put three coherent words together. This person was a drug addict.

I hesitantly followed him from the bathroom into the kitchen. Addison had a sweet tooth, and it began in the morning with a glass of homemade chocolate milk containing more Hershey's syrup than actual milk. To my amazement, he did manage to get the red Dixie cup turned right side up, though most of the milk and chocolate syrup ended up on the counter. He grabbed a dirty spoon from the sink to give it a rough stir as I crinkled my nose and turned my face away. I watched him pick up his backpack and stumble over the bodies of his friends still passed out on the floor. They were completely unaware of our presence. When we reached the car, I slung open the passenger door and exclaimed to our father, "He doesn't need orientation. He needs REHAB!" And oh, how right I was. I had *no idea* how right I was, but our visit to Room One that very same night in the hospital proved it.

family tradition

Addison's overdose on Xanax was on January 6 of 2009. I was 29 years old, and up to that point my life was, well, pretty marvelous. My mother would describe her life up to that point much differently. She was raised in a household riddled with drugs and alcoholism and watched her biological father abuse and terrorize her mother on a regular basis. My mother's childhood was by no means tranquil. She escaped at age eighteen by marrying my father whom she met in middle school. She continued to love him with her whole heart for the next 45 years.

My father had his own struggles with alcohol abuse, as did his father, who was a Full Commander in the Navy and died at age 41 from cirrhosis of the liver, and his grandfather, a pharmacist, who also died young. As a child, my mother lived in a constant state of fear, anxiety, and uncertainty. When I was little, I knew nothing of such trials. My mother made damn sure of it.

I did overhear my parents arguing, but what child doesn't? In my household, it was always the same argument. Like nails on a chalkboard, she would yell, "You've been drinking!" I couldn't decide whether the familiar sentence was a question or an accusation. She could tell if my father had been drinking just by glancing at him. He would inevitably try to tell her she was crazy, deny it to the core, but she knew better. His lazy eye (that my brother and I both inherited) appeared after only a few drinks and gave Dad away every time.

I heard this argument so many times that my response became a smug, "Here she goes again." In my childish eyes, I couldn't understand why she was always giving him such a hard time. He wasn't angry or violent when he drank. I was never afraid of my father, never embarrassed, never nervous to have my friends over to spend the night; what was the big deal? My dad is and has always been a kind and loving man.

What I couldn't comprehend then, yet do understand now, was my mother's desperate need to protect. The absence of shielding from the turmoil and destruction created in the tumultuous lifestyle she experienced as a child of an alcoholic, had yielded an exaggerated tendency to comfort and reassure. No one protected her, so she protected all of us. Thanks to Mom's efforts, the memories of my own childhood are predominantly filled with blissful times and contentment.

There is no doubt I was spoiled. I began riding horses when I was seven years old, which immediately became my passion and continues as a constant in my adult life. From the blustery winter days in the off-season to the blistering summer afternoons spent competing, I am my happiest when horses are near. The bond that exists between girl and horse is genuine, almost tangible, and I was obsessed with horses from the day of my very first lesson.

I have owned several ponies and horses in my lifetime, but my current horse, Cleo, is my love. She is a dainty little 15.3 hands, dark bay, thoroughbred mare, with long slender legs and a large white star adorning her refined head. She is striking and intuitive, with soft, kind eyes and a pleasant disposition. It always makes me smile when she appears delighted to see me arrive. More times than not she will notice my gold Suburban as I approach the driveway next to her paddock. She lets a huge welcoming whinny, and on those days, I find her ready to ride and happily waiting to greet me at the gate. Whether I am grooming her before or after a lesson, bathing her before heading off to a show, or just sitting with her in the field and watching her graze, she soothes my soul.

I am forever grateful for the day my mother asked me, "Would you like to take horseback riding lessons?" She expected that I would enjoy it because the love of all things equine runs in the family. What my parents offered me quickly became so much more than a hobby. It taught me a strong sense of responsibility from a very young age. Riding enabled me to continually strive to improve while harvesting my competitive nature. Riding became a part of me.

I vividly remember my mother surprising me on the occasional Thursday evening by telling me that I could miss a portion of the following school day to go to the barn to prepare for my weekend horse show. My nine-year-old voice would squeal with excitement. My parents were spontaneous, and I think that is one of the qualities that I like about them most. I can remember the three of us pulling up to the bank one afternoon. When you live in the South, you become acquainted with your teller, your pharmacist, your drycleaner, and so on, and you chit chat with them on each and every visit, however brief. The bank teller told my parents that she had just returned from a wonderful beach trip. When we pulled out of the parking lot, my mother said, "Hmmm, the beach sounds good."

To which my father replied, "You wanna go? Let's go." So, we went. We drove home, we packed our bags, and we headed to Myrtle Beach, South Carolina, for the entire week. My parents were fun like that.

In the winter of 1989, before my tenth birthday, we all got a big surprise. After years of trying and several miscarriages, my mother was pregnant. Oh, how I had begged for a baby brother or sister, and now I was going to have one! I told everyone—my friends at school, at the barn, my teacher. I completely disregarded my parents' instructions not to share the news just yet. When Addison arrived, he was perfect, and he looked sun-kissed straight out of the womb. I had spent nine months anxiously awaiting his arrival, watching my mother's belly grow, touching it, and talking and singing to him. He was born Monday night, October 24, two days before my tenth birthday. What a perfect birthday present!

I am uncertain how Addison would describe his own childhood memories. The circumstances were as idyllic as my own. Our home life was happy, my father had joined an International Bible Study and quit drinking, we went to church regularly, and we vacationed in the Bahamas at Christmas, which we all looked forward to every year. Addison and I had the same loving parents. He had our mother, who doted on him constantly, our father, who provided for us everything we could have ever wanted, and he had me, whom he followed relentlessly, like my little shadow. I welcomed his presence, he was always by my side, and I loved him. Though there was a decade between us, I still remember playing hide and seek and sliding down the stairs, together, in a large cardboard box. I taught him how to tie his shoes, ride his bike, and plunge off the diving board into the swimming pool in our backyard.

Though our circumstances were basically the same, Addison was very different from me. He was a chatterbox who could never focus, and he struggled in school. He cared much more about socializing than studying, and often made fun of me and called me a nerd. I had a small group of very close friends and tried to please my parents and teachers. Addison was very popular and was friends with everyone. I cried at the thought of a *B* on my report card, and Addison celebrated the thought of just passing. I was calm and creative and could easily entertain myself as a child, while Addison was wild, hyperactive, and demanded attention 24 hours a day. Even our outward appearances were opposites. My green eyes, and fair, freckled complexion were topped with a mop of natural, Shirley Temple curls that I despised. Addison charmed everyone with his beautiful dark brown eyes, olive skin, and densely thick straight hair which I envied. I resembled my mother's family and Addison was the spitting image of my father's. I used to joke that we didn't even look related.

At fifteen Addison was diagnosed with ADHD, which gave my parents some answers regarding his behavior and performance in school, but by then he had developed a complex. Though he was extremely quick witted and could think fast on his feet, inside he felt stupid and ill-equipped, and would often say that he would never measure up to me. Thinking back on how he must have felt, constantly comparing himself to my overachieving perfectionism, hurts my heart. When his diagnostician told him that actually he was quite gifted, with an IQ of 143, he was in disbelief. His exact response was "You expect me to believe that my whole life I have felt like the village idiot and now you're trying to tell me I'm boy genius?" That unabashed wittiness was my favorite thing about him.

Addison was put on medication for his ADHD, which was more difficult than it sounds. It took several different attempts to get the right combination of medications to work adequately for him. Overnight, he changed from a struggling straight *C* student, to a solid *A* student without having to crack a book. While on his medication, he discovered that he had a nearly photographic memory and could channel that into success with last minute studying, but unfortunately, like many medications, there were side effects. The medicine definitely made him focus, which made him quiet, something I never got accustomed to. Because he would never agree to wake at an early hour to take his medication, he had a very difficult time sleeping, which made him irritable. It took away his appetite, and even though his palate was limited, he missed being hungry.

I don't believe it was very long after his diagnosis of ADHD that Addison began experimenting with marijuana. Whether it was his own attempt to settle his incessantly racing ADHD mind or simply typical teenage, pot-smoking experimentation, I will never know. Though illegal, and definitely not condoned by my parents, the occasional joint did not seem to negatively affect him. When he was eighteen, he found an alternative that undeniably affected him. Well actually, it found him and it affected, no, it *infected* us all, and our lives were never the same.

quality time

Mother's Day in May of 2009 was no different than any other Mother's Day I had enjoyed since I was barely ten. I was at horse show that weekend. There were horse shows nearly every weekend from the first of April until the first weekend in November. In our East Tennessee Hunter Jumper Association, the Mother's Day weekend show is held at Walnut Grove Stables in Morristown, Tennessee, my favorite show venue in our circuit. The weekend competition had gone splendidly in my favor. The weather was sunny and mild with a light breeze making the usual "hurry up and wait" atmosphere very pleasant, especially since, at this point in my riding career, I usually rode very late into the afternoon and sometimes into the evening. Cleo and I had performed beautifully on Saturday, and the judge had fairly awarded us for our efforts. It was another delightful weekend of riding and showing, glorious weather, chilidogs and BBQ, and quality time with my horse, my trainer, and my friends.

    I was awakened by the sound of a bubbling coffee pot that Mother's Day morning. I had slept on the pullout couch, which I shared with one of my best friends, Michele, in the middle of Miss Dene's log cabin living room. The cabin was our lodging for the weekend show. Within moments the alarm began to beep, alerting us to each truck and trailer that pulled into the show grounds' driveway. I reminded myself to unplug the sensor when I went to bed there before the next show. I attempted, in vain, to return to sleep as people stirred and prepared for the show day. Because I refuse to unnecessarily get up before first light, I remained and snoozed off and on until I could procrastinate no longer. Around 9:30 that morning, I dressed and headed down toward the show barn to feed Cleo her breakfast and throw her a flake of hay. I gave her a quick brush and removed the shavings from her tail from her own night of stall slumber. I then headed up toward the show ring to assess the day's progress.

It was nearly four o'clock before I descended to the show barn again to prepare to ride. I changed into my show clothes in my truck, like many riders did, brushed and tacked Cleo, and headed for the warm-up ring. Fifteen minutes later, Michele, who was not only my friend and bed companion, but also the secretary and announcer for the show, had called all 2'6" Special Hunters to the in-gate. My trainer Melissa had put Cleo and me into our usual eight classes for the day. I was feeling confident as I entered the ring for my eighth and final class, since I had won the entire seven classes prior. I was halfway finished with what was turning out to be another lovely course when everything changed.

Nothing was amiss as I approached fence number five, The Wishing Well. I could see my distance from about six strides out. Our timing was perfect until, in an instant, I knew I was in trouble. Cleo tripped; in the immediate stride before we were to take off, Cleo uncharacteristically stumbled. There was nothing I could do. I was on the back of an eleven-hundred-pound animal who was about to nosedive to the sand below. Her front feet and legs crashed through the top two poles of the fence, breaking them in half like toothpicks. Immediately, her head dropped, her front end plummeted, and I was being drug down with her. I fell off on her right side and was momentarily knocked unconscious. After bursting through the top half of the fence, Cleo landed on her knees, face-planting her nose into the footing of the ring. She scrambled, valiantly attempting to leave me unscathed, but in the midst of our landing her right hind foot came crashing down onto my back.

When I came to, I was disoriented, I had a mouthful of sand, I couldn't breathe, and the crushing pain on the left side of my back was unbearable. Among those who came rushing to my aid were Melissa, the judge, who had leapt from his perch in the judge's booth, and Bonnie, a doctor and the mother of a young competitor at the show. Bonnie was taking my pulse and trying to calm me while Melissa whipped out her Mother of Pearl pocketknife and sliced up the slide of my sports bra through the giant rip in my shirt to help me catch my breath. "Where, is, Cleo?" I grunted. "Cleo is fine, Jess. I need you to breathe in through your nose and out through your mouth," Bonnie kept repeating. "She smokes a pack a day Bonnie, she can't do that," Melissa answered in her own, raspy, two pack-a-day smoker's voice. "You're going to have to try and get calmer, slower breaths in, Jess. Your pulse is almost at 200," explained Bonnie. Oh, I wanted to get my breath back. I just kept telling myself that when I could get my breath back under control I was going to get back on my horse, despite how badly I was hurting.

As I gasped for air I managed to ask if someone could bring me a rag to get the sand and tiny pieces of gravel out of my mouth. I struggled to sit up when I heard the crunch. I collapsed in defeat and stared up at Melissa. "My ribs are broken," I whispered. "I don't know how many, but it's bad. Is Cleo okay?"

"She's fine Jess," Melissa answered. "Ally has her. She broke your reins, but she's fine."

"Are you sure?" I kept on.

Melissa chuckled, "I'm sure; in fact, once she got to her feet she went on and jumped the next jump without you!"

Once they convinced me that my horse was not injured, I resolved to lie still and focus on breathing until the ambulance arrived; I cried on the inside because I knew my show season was over.

It was a ten-mile trip by ground ambulance to the local Hamblen County Hospital, where a helicopter was waiting to airlift me to the Trauma Center at UT Hospital. Melissa had called my parents after the accident, and they were there waiting for me by the time the chopper touched down. I received 17mg of morphine while in the helicopter, which made me inebriated but did little to ease my pain. Upon arrival, the trauma team surrounded me, stripped me of my riding clothes, and rushed me off for X-rays and CT scans. Though my left lung had not collapsed, it did suffer a minor puncture, and I had seven broken ribs to go along with it.

After one sleepless night in the hospital on a Dilaudid drip, I was released to return home for my estimated six to eight-week recovery. Naturally, I was taken straight to my parents' house because that is where every sick, injured, or post-surgical family member or friend ended up. With her adjustable Tempur-Pedic bed in the master bedroom on the main floor, my mother made recovering from anything as comfortable as possible because caring for others is what she did best. Being tended to by the world's greatest caregiver was not my only respite from my unfortunate situation; Addison was home. Fresh out of rehab and anxiously awaiting me at the back door was my sleepy-eyed little brother. Wagging at his feet was his therapy dog, Sadie, a shiny black Labrador puppy that he had brought home from treatment. He greeted me with a gentle hug, careful not to squeeze my broken body, and he winced right along with me at each and every labored shallow breath as he helped me to our parents' bed. He went to his room and returned with his favorite feather pillow and UT orange fleece blanket and took his place beside me, along with Sadie, just as he had done as a little boy.

While my mother scurried here and there cooking and cleaning, getting my prescriptions filled, and making her 10,000th run to the grocery store for yet another gallon of milk, Addison and I lay and talked. Though we had spoken every Friday evening during our ten-minute family phone calls, and we had visited him on a couple of occasions, he wanted to reiterate his experiences in Nowhere, Arkansas. The discomfort of rehab, the cold crappy cabin, and the lumpy bed. I heard about it all. He grumbled about the strict rules and regulations placed upon him, including the nicotine patch they slapped on his arm moments after tossing his Marlboro 27's in the garbage. He told me about all the other guys that he met, what their issues were, and their personal drugs of choice. I got the backstory on the therapists that he bonded with, learned about the friends he made, and heard all about how horrible the food he was "forced to eat."

I told him about how torturous it had been for me during his time away was, as if he hadn't already realized that from the countless letters I wrote to him on a nightly basis when sleep wouldn't come. I recounted about manning his cell phone 24 hours a day to ward off the constant pill solicitation from his fellow drug compadres. I made him help me decipher their drug lingo, which was like cracking the Da Vinci Code, and told him how I had threatened all his drug friends within an inch of their lives if they ever called him again, which, surprisingly, he thought was hilarious. He threw his head back and laughed, making his most famous statement about me. "Don't fuck with my sister," he chuckled. We talked about his plans for the upcoming semester at UT and what he would pick for his major. Addison had always longed to be like our dad, who is a certified public accountant and financial planner. Thus, Addison decided to major in business administration, ignoring that I had minored in business and assured him that he would hate it. He would later change it, giving me another opportunity to tell him, "I told you so."

Over the next four weeks my parents' bedroom was transformed into our own little world. We talked, we laughed, we took naps, and we played with the new puppy. Daily, I threatened to make him leave the room if he didn't stop making me laugh until I literally cried from the pain of my fractured ribs. We had nightly card tournaments of Canasta and Spades with our mother, and she routinely persuaded us into Chinese checkers, which she always won. Sam made frequent visits to check on me and occasionally brought one of our dogs. Addison and I hogged the remote from everyone, and by the end of my stay we had watched the full six seasons of *House* on DVD.

When the time came for me to return to my own house, Addison begged me not to go. Knowing it was impossible and unrealistic, he still turned his face downcast, jutted out his bottom lip, and, like a child, asked, "Do you really have to go home? Why can't you and Sam just move in here and we all live together? Please don't leave. I want you to stay here with me." Such a large part of me felt his pain. Though I wanted to go home to my husband, my own house, and my dogs, it proved difficult to leave him. We had had such a good time together, quality time, time that made me miss all of the years before I had gotten married, time during which we lived in the same house together, time which made me forget that my horse show season for that year was all but in the toilet, time that, years later, I would do anything to get back.

big A

Addison's nickname from as far back as I can remember was *Big A*, which is funny because he was never a big kid; it was his personality that was super-sized. I can still see him at barely two years old bopping and swaying on his uncoordinated, chunky baby legs to the irresistible sound of the steel drum band in the customs line at the Nassau, Bahamas, airport. He was blissfully unaware of the other vacationers giggling and whispering among themselves and sometimes to my parents about how unequivocally adorable he was. He was always impulsive, and even as a very small child, when he heard music he couldn't help but dance.

On another Nassau vacation, when Addison was eleven, he excused himself from the dinner table to use the restroom. At least that is what we all assumed. When he did not return in a reasonable span of time, my slightly concerned parents sent me searching. Barely able to breathe from laughter, I returned to the table and motioned for my parents to follow me. From the second floor of the restaurant we could hear the Caribbean version of "Limbo Rock" resonating from the band below. There in the middle of the limbo line was nine-year-old Addison doing the limbo with half a dozen tipsy out-of-towners and a handful of fun-loving Bahamian natives. When he finally made his way back to the table, he appeared slightly winded. His response to our laughter was a coy, "Sorry, I just heard it, and I couldn't help it."

Whatever part of Addison's personality that would compel him to do such things is probably the same part of his personality that everyone was drawn toward. He was magnetic, radiating in charisma and oozing with charm. The environment he created around him was teeming with friends from every walk of life; he discriminated against no one and was heard on a number of occasions declaring, "You just don't understand. I AM the crowd!" He appeared to be everyone's favorite. During his kindergarten parent/teacher meet and greet, there were three mothers who boldly stated that their child was happy to be in Ms. "So and So's" class because Addison was there.

He just had that way about him that made everyone love him right from the start, and as he grew older he learned to use it to his advantage. I don't know many college students who could convince a professor to adjust a test score by simply saying, "I know that I got an 88, but couldn't I have a 92?" Addison could. He was incredibly persuasive, and with one look from those big puppy dog eyes he could melt a heart. Countless times I was suckered into making my creamed mashed potatoes for him when I neither had the time nor the ingredients on hand. He asked one question, "Jessica, how much do you love me?" I was keenly aware that I was being manipulated, but it always worked.

Though cunning, Addison had a heart of gold. He was kind and compassionate, almost hypersensitive to the feelings of others. Though he ran with the popular crowd in school, he was also a friend to the friendless, always the first to introduce himself to the new kid who had not yet found his or her place. He made others feel welcomed. He was generous to a fault, a trait that was undeniably inherited from our mother. Whether it was CDs, video games, clothing, or cold hard cash, Addison was always giving or loaning out his belongings with little concern for their return.

Addison was also very strong in his faith from an unusually young age. He would often verbally spar with his Catholic High School teachers about beliefs they held that differed from our Presbyterian upbringing. He regularly attended youth group at our church and went on mission trips to Rock Sound on the island of Eleuthera, in the Bahamas.

He was not embarrassed or ashamed to share with others what he believed. At age ten, he burst through the back door of my parents' house one humid summer afternoon in hot pursuit of our mother's ear. "Mom! Mama! MOTHER!" he yelled.

"In here!" she screamed back in an irritable tone.

Her mood immediately lightened when she heard Addison exclaim, "He believes! He believes, Mom!"

"Who believes? What are your talking about?" she asked

"David! I converted him!" Addison beamed as he bounced up and down with excitement. My mother had seen Addison and the neighborhood boy, David, standing at the end of the driveway together for some time that afternoon, having no idea that Addison was preaching to the kid. "I told him all about the gospel and about who Jesus is, and that all he had to do was to accept Him and believe, and then he would have eternal life, and he did, and I converted him!" he proclaimed.

Several weeks later, when Addison saw David again, he came looking for our mother but this time with tears in his eyes. "He said he was lying," Addison pouted.

"Who's lying?" she asked.

"David! He lied. He doesn't believe. He said he was lying that day when I talked to him and that he actually doesn't believe anything." Addison cried. Our mother consoled her little evangelist, reassuring him that it wasn't his responsibility to save people because Jesus was the only one who could save. We were responsible only to plant the seed. The following week Addison came inside from playing and said, "Well, I saw David, and I worked on planting that seed again, and, well, I think it took this time."

Because of his passion, my mother used to tell Addison that he should become a pastor. He could have just as easily, however, harnessed his boisterous comedic flair into a career. The kid was just plain funny. Wherever he was, Addison made people laugh. He had the ability to shift any downhearted or depressed mood or to diffuse an argument with one perfectly placed and brilliantly witted statement, like when my mother finally did spank him with that wooden spoon she had been threatening him with for days if he did not stop whining. When the old and half-rotten utensil broke in half over his little butt cheeks, he simply turned to her, smiled, and said, "Buns of Steel," giggling as he walked away.

Several years later, while riding in the back seat of Sam's Honda Civic and listening to Sam and me scream at each other during one of our many young lover's quarrels, Sam turned to Addison and sighed, "I tell ya, Addison, women, you can't live with them, and you can't live without them."

To which Addison replied, "I know! How are we supposed to eat?" Those are just a couple of what seems like hundreds of stored up, treasured memories of the laughter that he brought into everyone's life.

It is hard for me to reconcile those precious memories of Addison with what drugs ultimately made him become. At his core, I know he was still that same sweet, sensitive, kind, and fun-loving kid whom everyone adored. Outwardly, however, his behaviors, which became driven by almost primal motivations, began to deteriorate across time and manifest themselves in ways that even he thought were unimaginable. Though he continued to coast through life with humor and maintained his multitude of friendships, there was a darkness and the possibility that every word he spoke to us was a lie behind his beautiful eyes.

He became tortured through his constant internal battle between good and evil as he tried to hide his struggle and pain behind laughs and smiles. Addison was home from rehab for about six months before his first relapse. Unfortunately, not only did he relapse with benzodiazepines like Xanax, but also his "friends" were all too eager to help him upgrade to opiates when the benzos just didn't seem to cut it anymore, and Roxicet soon became his newest demon.

The next two years were a roller coaster for us all. Addison bounced from my parents' house, to several new apartments, to my grandparents' house and back again. His weight fluctuated just as rapidly, depending on his varying degrees of sobriety. He went from a healthy 180 pounds down to a frighteningly skeletal 135 pounds. His already melodramatic temperament became increasingly erratic as he exhibited irrational mood swings and exaggerated crises. Lying became his native tongue and stealing from my parents his second nature. His charisma and charm that we loved so much became weapons of manipulation he used against us on a daily basis. He became a master of deception and lived a secret life, much of which we knew nothing about. Surprisingly, he was able to maintain his good grade point average at UT and continued to laugh and smile, which made his elaborate stories and excuses all the more plausible.

When you love an addict, you believe the lies, you deny the truth, and some small part of you thinks that if you just pray enough, do enough, and love him enough, everything will turn out okay. You just have to fight hard enough and never give up. You have to believe to personally survive the trauma; otherwise, you are left feeling powerless and hopeless. Addison never wanted us to lose our faith that he could overcome his battle, but it became more and more difficult to calm our fears when his closest friends began to die.

On a blustery day in early December of 2011, I stood arm in arm with my brother on a grassy hillside among his classmates just three years out of high school and watched as they laid one of his best friends into the ground. He fought back tears in an attempt to be strong, but from our close proximity I could feel his body quaking with sorrow. When the service concluded, Addison and I stood together beside his friend's casket. I turned to him, grabbed his arms, and looked up into his eyes. I said, "All I can tell you Addison is that if THAT were you, I would die. Do you hear me?" I asked as I gently shook him and tears streamed down my face. "I could NOT deal with that. I would never make it. If you died, it would be my death, too." Because we were alone, he finally did release the flood of tears that he had been choking back throughout the entire service.

He looked back at me with concern and said what he always said to me, "Don't worry about me, okay? Please, don't worry. I can't stand you worrying about me. I'll be okay."

Oh, how I wanted to believe him every time he assured me that he would be okay, just as I wanted to believe him every time he lied to my face. The anguish that built up inside of me for the little brother that I loved so much, yet was powerless to help, came rushing out in waves. Many nights I tried flushing it out with alcohol, which I'm sure seems just as self-destructive as Addison's behavior, but there were days when I just couldn't deal. I drank to excess just to numb my worries and my fears, but it somehow never seemed to deliver the desired effect. What I was attempting to use to make me forget my suffering only fueled my affliction until I became a hysterical tornado of helplessness and rage prone to screaming and breaking things. "Why won't God just make him better? God needs to either HEAL him or just let him DIE!" I would wail. It's hard to believe that you could love someone that much, yet allow fear, anxiety, and heartache to push you to the point of saying something so horrible.

In my heart, I was never wishing for my brother's death. I just wanted our nightmare to be over. I longed for the simpler times of the past when we were kids, when the issues that I worried about were trivial. I wanted to return to the days when my heart didn't stop and skip two beats at the sound of the telephone ringing for fear that something else awful had happened. I wanted to be able to call or text my brother and not worry that he had been arrested or was lying unconscious somewhere just because he didn't answer or text me back right away. I wanted to believe him when he spoke to me. Every day I lived in fear that I would lose him. I just wanted it to stop. I wanted my brother back.

There were sober days, weeks, and sometimes months during which the *Big A* I remembered was back to his old self, but I learned that those peaks were always followed by valleys, and there was nothing I could do to stop the cycle.

twenty-two

I awoke on the morning of January 2, 2012, dreading the day. We had returned home the night before from another Christmas in the Bahamas, and I had to unpack (one of my least favorite activities). It was time to put away my bathing suits and flip-flops and trade them in for boots and scarves for three more dreary winter months. We had a wonderful trip, and the adjustment of not having Jim with us was easier than I had expected. Jim and Susie were two of my parents' best friends. For many years, basically a decade, they accompanied us on our Christmas vacations. The 2012 trip was our first holiday back on the island following Jim and Susie's unfortunate divorce, and I wondered how the dynamics of our group would change with that missing link, yet somehow things still seemed quite normal even in the midst of Jim's absence.

Coming home from the warmth of the Nassau sun still saddened me even though everything else in my world seemed to be looking up. For six solid months Addison had been clean, which was evident by, among other things, his nearly 40-pound weight gain. The brightness had returned to his eyes, and he looked healthy again with his freshly buzzed haircut and his carefully manicured little beard that I used to joke made him look like Abraham Lincoln. He seemed optimistic about returning to UT that Wednesday and was excited about his major change to psychology. Following his stint in rehab, Addison decided to become a psychologist, proving my accurate prediction that he would despise the world of business administration.

Though for the most part he looked back on his experience in treatment as positive, his main complaint was that his therapist had never been an addict. "Don't get me wrong," he would say, "Jeremiah was a super nice guy, and I really liked him, but he didn't GET IT. He's never struggled with this demon, and no amount of schooling can make you understand what an addict goes through every minute of every day. I've actually been there. I know what it's like. If I become a counselor, there is no telling how many people I can help." It was in Addison's nature to help others since he was a small child, so no one was surprised at his desire to use his experiences to serve the suffering.

I piddled in the bathroom, sleepily putting away my toiletries and then followed that with my Red Bull and cigarette breakfast of champions. Sam was in his office when his cell phone rang around 9:30 that morning. I paid no attention, assuming it was one of his patients or his sister. Suddenly, Sam appeared in the bathroom doorway. The look on his face was unfamiliar. "It's Addison. You need to get dressed." A powerful flood of adrenaline shot shockwaves to my bones.

"WHY? What happened? Who was that?" I asked, my eyes instantly filling with tears.

"It was Susie. We need to get to Baptist Hospital."

I know that as my quivering hands were fumbling for something to wear, I repeatedly asked him what was wrong. I screamed, "What happened? What's wrong? What did she say?" The only response he would give me was that we just needed to get there.

The short drive to the hospital seemed to take an eternity. I questioned Sam for the entirety of the drive, and in my heart I knew he was holding something back. I screamed at him as I violently rocked myself back and forth. I was nearly unable to control myself.

"She said it was something to do with his heart," he finally replied. His vague answer left me with only further questions.

"What about his heart? What happened? Is he going to die? We just got home! I just saw him last night! He was FINE! What is happening?" I was frantic, sweating, my heart was pounding, and we couldn't seem to get there fast enough. Once again all I could do was pray, "Please don't let him die, God. PLEASE!"

I burst through the emergency room doors, my face flushed red with tears that streamed down my cheeks. My attention was immediately directed to the small room to my left where I saw Orbin standing in the doorway. I ran to him with Sam in close pursuit. Behind Orbin, seated in a wheelchair in the corner, was my mother, dressed in nothing but her black winter overcoat covering her pajamas. Her gaze was fixed on her tiny quivering hands that held a well-used Kleenex. As I exploded into the windowless, claustrophobic room, she looked up at me with her big blue eyes that were now filled with indescribable pain. "HE'S DEAD!"

I will never forget that moment; as hard as I try to erase the worst day of my life, the memory will not leave me. The sound of the scream that escaped from my lips in that moment did not sound human. My legs collapsed beneath me, but Orbin and Sam caught the weight of my body before

I hit the floor. I was trapped in their simultaneous bear hug as my body writhed and seized against their equally strong grips. "LET ME GO! LET GO OF ME! LET GOOOOO!" I screamed. They released me, and I scrambled back to my feet, peeling off the layers of my sweater and long-sleeved shirt now stuck to my skin with sweat. I felt as if my body would explode as I paced the tiny room like a caged animal shouting in disbelief, "NO! NO! NO! This isn't happening! This ISN'T happening!!!"

I can remember wanting to pick up the wooden chairs upholstered in cheap imitation leather and lining the tiny death room and smash them through the drywall. What stopped me was seeing my mother, with her hands covering her face because the sight of my reaction was more than she could bear. I fell to the floor once again and crawled to my tiny mother on my hands and knees. I wrapped my arms around her feeble frame and laid my head in her lap and sobbed, "Oh Mama, NO! NO!" I cried. I could feel her body shaking, quaking with sorrow, and then I heard my dad. I had never seen my dad cry, at least, not like this. He was seated in a chair up against the wall, dressed in his jeans and brown leather jacket. I turned from my mother and crawled to his feet, and somehow managed to fold my entire 5'7" frame into his lap like a little girl. "Oh Dad, NO!" I cried as he held me like a child and he sobbed. There was nothing anyone could do to console any of us, and there is nothing more heartbreaking than seeing your father sob uncontrollably, helplessly.

We must have looked despondent sometime later, when we were once again led to Room One to see my brother. Arm in arm, we leaned on each other as we hesitantly maneuvered our way down the short corridor to that cold and dreaded space in the left corner of the emergency room.

I had become all too familiar with that room, the same room that they had ushered me into years earlier when Addison suffered his first overdose. The last time I approached this room I saw my brother all groggy, droopy-eyed, and furious at me, but he was alive, and that was all that mattered. Now as I approached, I was faced with an unimaginable horror. The fear that I had expressed to him one year and one month before to the day at his friend's funeral had become my reality.

Nurses had placed a small black chair at his side for my mother, who the hospital staff knew would not be able to stand. With my parents on his left side, and Sam and me on his right, we stared at my baby brother's lifeless body. Twenty-two. Twenty-two years old and he was gone. My eyes scanned the length of his 5'10" frame that just the evening before had seemed so full of life. He was dressed as my mother had found him that morning—in his boxer shorts and hunter green Catholic High School bowling team T-shirt. Of course, he was the captain of the bowling team. We touched him and his hands, with his little fingernails he had meticulously bitten down to the quick. His arms, which were so full of warmth only twelve hours ago when he hugged me goodbye in my driveway, now cold and limp. His face, the light now completely gone from those beautiful eyes, now blank and half open, still adorned with those long, dark lashes. His mouth was partially open revealing a small glimpse of the dental veneers that my husband had placed and that Addison was so proud of. There was a tiny hair strewn across his pretty new teeth that had obviously fallen from the head of a paramedic, or nurse, or doctor trying to save his life. It bothered me terribly that there was someone else's hair in his mouth, and so I removed it ever so gently. My mother and I clung to each of his hands and kissed his fingers and his cheeks. We hovered over his body, sobbing in sorrow, washed in disbelief. How could this have happened?

My father bent over and kissed his forehead and whispered to him something that only I was close enough to hear, "I'm so sorry I did this to you." His guilt broke me. Knowing the strong ties between addiction and genetics, my father was already blaming himself.

My mother had found Addison in his room that morning when she went to wake him so that he could go pick up Sadie from the vet. His body was already cold to the touch at 9:00 a.m. that morning. He had died in the middle of the night and had been gone far too long for any major organ donation, but they asked us if they could take his eyes. His eyes were the only parts of him that were still viable for donation so long after death. Of course, we agreed; those eyes were the most beautiful physical things about him. It gave us the slightest amount of comfort when we received the thank you letter months later stating that Addison's beautiful eyes had been successfully donated and that because of him, a blind person had been given the gift of sight. Deep down I have always wanted to meet that person. I feel connected to him, this stranger walking around with my brother's eyes.

We all experienced another wave of panic when we were told that the transport had arrived to take Addison's body for autopsy. We knew it was time to say goodbye. I didn't want to let him go. My mother, of course, didn't want to let him go. None of us knew how on earth we would go on. How could we continue in this life without *Big A*? He was my treasure, my one and only brother, and 22 years seemed like such a short time. I leaned over his face one last time and kissed him just as I had done the night before. One of my tears landed on his cheek and I watched it trickle down the side of his face. I said the same words to him that I had said the night before, and in that instant, I was at least grateful that the last words I ever spoke to him in life and in death were, "I love you."

aftermath

"Please eat this. Just one bite. Will you please just take one bite? For me?" One of my mother's best friends, Wanda, was seated next to me on my parents' gold and black upholstered sofa. She held half of a chicken salad sandwich to my face and begged me to eat. I couldn't stomach even the thought of food. None of us could. My lack of nutrition would show in a month's time. I looked awful. Darkness began to encircle my hollowed-out eyes. I went days upon days without taking a shower and didn't care or even notice. By the time I was convinced that I was in desperate need of some personal hygiene, there were portions of my Shirley Temple curls that had begun to mat together in a tangled mess of confusion. Then my hair started falling out altogether.

My 5'7" slender, yet muscular 110-pound frame had withered away to a frail and feeble 95 pounds of skin and bone. I survived on a steady flow of caffeine and nicotine, and far too often, alcohol for good measure. It ceased to bother me to walk into a gas station, grocery store, or liquor store in a pair of baby pink and black polka dot flannel pajamas, which had become my uniform. I lashed out at anyone who said something (that I usually misconstrued) in an attempt to help. No one could help me. I lost friends who couldn't or wouldn't handle my grief because they could not begin to comprehend the pain. I made a handful of my remaining friends cry on at least one occasion because when I ran out of tears, my only other emotional outlet was to scream. I was delirious in the aftermath of Addison's sudden death. It is hard to fully describe the days, weeks, and months in the wake of such tragedy, mainly; the memories are few.

"I can't believe I'm putting this on for my brother," I said, as I dressed in my black Ann Taylor skirt suit that had mainly been reserved for funerals, and, incidentally, I have never worn again. Our church was packed to near capacity with close to 500 people in attendance at Addison's memorial service on the 5th of January. At the front of the church stood two perfectly manicured topiaries. Between them was an easel holding a life-sized color portrait of Addison in his tux. It was his senior yearbook photo. On the corner of the picture frame hung a flat-billed baseball hat that he never left home without. I don't remember much of what our pastors said during Addison's service, but I do remember that I was unable to cry. I was three days in, and the shock was still so great that not only was I able to walk up on stage in front of hundreds of people and sing Sarah McLachlan's "I Will Remember You," without faltering, but I also was able to sit through my baby brother's funeral without shedding one tear. It was surreal. *Perhaps*, I thought, *this isn't really happening.* I kept hoping that it was just a horrible nightmare.

There was no casket. We decided to have Addison cremated because we didn't want to live at the cemetery. My mother and I knew that if we placed Addison's body in the ground, even though we knew it was only his body and that he was no longer there, that we would haunt the cemetery for an unknown and extended period of time. We hated the notion that there could be a location to "go to." Even now when I drive past a cemetery, I thank God that we didn't bury him because it's not a place that I would wish to frequent; yet, I know that I would somehow feel an irrational sense of guilt for not regularly visiting. Our plan was to scatter his ashes in the crystal-clear turquoise waters of the Bahamas, our second home, but what seemed like a good idea in theory proved to be more difficult for my mother and my dad, and I never pushed.

We seemed trapped, for a period, in a permanent spin cycle of broken heartedness, misery, and grief. The immense trauma and shock affected each of us differently as we all had varying degrees of amnesia. My dad says that he lost a full year; whereas, I have bits and pieces of memory following Addison's death that become less fragmented beginning around the third or fourth month.

My mother, unfortunately, never seemed to even partially recover from the loss. I have no recollection of any local or world events that made the headlines during that time, and though I have disconnected memories of being at particular places, I have no concrete recall of my comings and goings or how I got from one place to another.

Because he is a CPA, January is the beginning of my dad's busiest season at work, tax season. He returned to work relatively soon, and even now neither he nor anyone else understands how he was able to do so. My mother took to her bed, rarely leaving the dark, quiet, safe space she had created for herself, and tried to convince her heart of what her mind already knew. Addison was home now.

We knew what Addison believed, and we knew that in His mercy, Christ had taken him home where he would no longer suffer the pain and anguish of addiction. We knew that we would see him again. We tried to rely on our faith, to let it give us hope and strength. "In my mind, I know it is right," she would say. "I know that God doesn't make mistakes, and I know that it was his time. I know that he was saved, and I know where he is. I just wish someone could make it be okay with my heart. I just miss him so badly it hurts every part of me." None of us could disagree, and because of that hope, my dad and I tried to push on, however slowly, but my mother, though full of wisdom, seemed to always lack the might.

My strength grew only with time, little by little, when each day came and went and the pain of losing him did not kill me. I found myself surprised that I didn't die, and many days I prayed that I would. I wanted to wake up in the morning and have my life back the way it was before. "Before and After" is how I began and continue to decipher time. Circumstances and life events either happened when Addison was alive or after he died. It was the most defining moment of my life, and yet the trauma of it has blocked out so much of my memory surrounding that time that his death is my only frame of reference for remembering those days, weeks, and months. Our whole world had changed in an instant, and we knew that none of us would ever be the same. There were just moments, mere milliseconds,= during the partial consciousness between sleep and wakefulness, that I would feel at peace each morning. Then it would hit me; Addison is gone. The thought would flood my heart with an unbearable ache chased by incredible anxiety that the reality of his death was now my life. Every morning, for months, I experienced this tidal wave of emotions that plunged me into despair before my feet ever hit the floor.

We were in the *haze*, as I call it, the haze of misery and grief during which days and nights run together. The haze is filled with only very few disjointed memories because time is no longer linear. For the first several weeks immediately following Addison's death we spent large portions of our days and nights huddled in his room, joined many times by some of Addison's closest high school friends. We could still smell him in his room. His clothes, hats, blankets, and pillows were still washed in that distinctive smell that each individual has, and my mother and I couldn't seem to tear ourselves away from his scent. I would curl up in his blanket and lie in his burgundy leather recliner where my mother had found him, the chair where he fell asleep and never woke up. Extended family and friends surrounded us for a time until they all left to naturally continue on with their lives, which was something that for us seemed impossible.

It was by far the most difficult time in all of our lives. The memories of my brother were inescapable, seeming to slap us in the face at every turn, and even the fond memories of him were incredibly painful. I could still hear his voice and his little boy laugh throughout the entire house. No matter where I went, or what I was doing, he was there. His memory haunted every step and reminded me that there were no more memories to be made.

I had difficulty in the coming months driving anywhere around town. I would pass Jets Pizza or Sam & Andy's Deli and think of him. I'd cry the whole way home after passing where he went to school, where our old Blockbuster Video building, where we picked out hundreds of movies together, used to be, all the apartments Addison had lived in and I'd helped load and load furniture into and out of, and, to my utmost frustration and rage, the place where my brother got his first job and met the "friend" who gave him the first pill that started this whole traumatic existence. The business closed down and was bulldozed. A hotel was erected in its place, but the location gives me a lingering and ironic combination of distress and contentment. No escape.

My mind wrestled with my inability to comprehend that he was really gone. I had *just* stood in my driveway and hugged him goodbye. I told him that I loved him, never knowing that it would be for the very last time.

"I love you" were the last words that Addison spoke to my parents as well.

About an hour after we got home from our vacation, he went to Sonic to pick up his usual: a grilled cheese sandwich and cheese tater tots. He sat on the end of their bed and talked while he ate, then kissed my mom on the cheek and headed to his room. We have always been thankful that "I love you" were all of our last words to Addison. Throughout his struggles with addiction there had been many conversations that had ended with "I hate you!" or some other derivative spoken out of anger and desperation. My mother said that the time that we spent with Addison during our last trip to the Bahamas, and the "Good nights" and "Goodbyes" that were filled with nothing but love were just another gift from God, who knew what was to come. It all could have ended so differently.

Though I knew that my mother was right on all accounts, I was angry. I was angry at the world because my brother was no longer in it. I was angry at a life that I was now forced to live without him. It took me quite a while to realize that I was angry with God, too, for taking my brother from me. I was angry that all of these young people were dying year after year, and no one appeared to have an explanation as to why or appeared to be doing anything about it. My family always assumed that Addison had simply gotten mixed up with the wrong crowd. Though we narrowed it down to a small list of suspects, we will never know which of his "friends" delivered the two pills of Opana to my parents' house late in the night. Before Addison's death we had never even heard of Opana.

My family had no idea of the plague that our culture was and is facing, nor that our own Tennessee was at the top of the list of states drowning in prescription pills, but I was about to get a full and comprehensive education on this topic. The journey that I was getting ready to embark upon would teach me more than I ever imagined. My laser focus on loving and grieving for my brother broadened to understanding addiction across generations and then fighting boundary-less, pervasive, pure evil of the world. The greatest journey of my life began. I didn't contemplate this journey before I started it. I was fueled by something deep within and really just reacted. It amazes me that in the midst of the most indescribable grief, I was able to coherently communicate. I climbed my first step, an email, just a few short days after Addison's death.

Looking back, I know now that God led me down the path I would follow for many years. I know that He helped me write that first email. God opened every door. God directed me to the right people at the right times and helped me articulately express myself in midst of personal trauma. God brought people I needed at the time and still immeasurably love to this day into my life.

The path was grueling. Many times, it seemed like a never-ending, uphill battle that I could never win, but like my mother said, "God doesn't make mistakes." God chose Addison, and then He chose me for this task. I'm not sure that I will ever know why.

david & goliath

I had no idea what I was getting myself into when I started. In the beloved Bible story, before David took down Goliath, he got a good look at Goliath and was able to size him up. Terrifying as it must have been, David didn't let fear stop him from taking down the giant who towered over him. At least David knew what he was up against. I was a little less informed about the battle I was about to face, but I didn't let that stop me from picking a fight. I'd like to say that I, initially, fully understood the physical struggle, the emotional labor, and the writhing mental effort that would be necessary for the path I soon took. I'd like to say that I wouldn't have chosen that road, but saying so would be dishonest. I was pissed. My whole world had just fallen apart, my heart shattered into a million pieces, and though I knew there was nothing on this earth that I could do to bring my baby brother back, I'd be damned if I was going to let it continue to happen while everyone else either stayed as uninformed as we had once been or continue to turn blind eyes to the relentless death and devastation caused by addition.

What was happening here? I thought. I was confused. I learned that the problem far exceeded the boundaries of my nuclear family, but the awful reality was hard to calculate and comprehend. To understand my perplexity, you have to understand where I live. Tennessee is a sprawling state. Of the roughly six and one-half million Tennesseans, approximately 850,000 live in Knoxville and the immediate surrounding areas. Addison and I grew up in the affluent town of Farragut, a suburb of Knoxville that straddles two neighboring counties and is home to a little more than 20,000 people. Even in the most populated of residential areas, we still have our own space. Houses are not jammed in on top of one another like in so many other massive metropolitan areas of the country. Whether it is winter, spring, summer, or fall, Tennessee is beautiful. Even though we are in the South, most people, except me (I could chuck winter altogether), appreciate the fact that we still have all four seasons. Tennessee is flush in rivers and lakes, rolling hills, and the unmatched Great Smoky Mountains. Tennessee is the birthplace of country music, the home of Elvis Presley and Dolly Parton, and the producer of Jack Daniel's Whiskey. I realize that my description sounds like the eloquent writings of your local motel lobby vacation guide, but that's the way I view my state. I love living in Tennessee.

Addison and I grew up in a very nice home that my parents built in the late 1980s. Though Farragut is a an enclave dotted with beautiful homes and manicured lawns, clean streets driven by expensive cars, well-attended churches, retail stores, and restaurants, my naiveté about our quaint little town made the reality of my blowing the lid off of our dirty little secret all the more sobering.

I always thought that truly bad things didn't happen in our town. Our town was safe. Our town was pretty. Yet something drastic had changed in our town, in our city, and in our state in just ten years' time. No one said anything about it because, after all, we're from the South. In the South, and especially in a place like Farragut, there are just certain things you didn't air to the general public. People would whisper about Mr. "So & So" down the street who had an affair with his secretary. I might hear about Mrs. "So & So" who had "a little drinking problem" and had an unfortunate and embarrassing run-in with the law. But I NEVER heard about the hundreds, and later, thousands of people (mostly teens and young adults), dropping dead on a daily basis from a drug overdoses. Right under our affluent noses, needless premature deaths were happening and no one talked about it. The obituary section in the newspaper began to read like little unsolved mysteries as it became more and more filled with the "sudden death" announcements of young and healthy-appearing high school and college students

 I didn't care what anybody thought. During the last four years of Addison's life, our family, including Addison, never hid the fact that he was an addict. I put him on the prayer list in Sunday school. All of our friends and family knew about his struggles. I could never understand how people could walk around in the world as though they were at a masquerade ball. Families have sad secrets and struggles, but people will look you right in the face and tell you that they are doing just fine, when in reality, they are fighting a battle that is privy to no one else. Because of their secrecy (and perhaps personal shame), they fight it alone. I've never understood fighting battles alone. How can you ask people to pray for you if no one knows what you are going through? How can you step outside and face the day as if you have not a care in the world, only to return home and suffer in silence? I've never had the ability to put on a mask and pretend that everything is fine, publicly or privately. Though

I might, and I mean, "might" be able to control my tongue at the appropriate times, there is no denying my facial expressions. All I can be is open and honest. I don't know any other way. I can't hide my emotions, good or bad, and I don't care what anybody thinks.

We were seated in my mother's buttercream yellow kitchen, chain-smoking, and still in our pajamas following another night of fitful sleep when I first brought it up. "Something is terribly wrong here," I said.

My mother looked at me like I had ten heads, "Uh, yeah!" she replied.

"No, I mean besides Addison, something is going on here. Something is wrong. This isn't normal," I said.

"What do you mean?" she asked.

"These kids are dying. All these young people in our town, in our *neighborhoods*, people we know, keep overdosing. I mean, I grew up here too. I went to school at UT, and I didn't bury my friends every year. These pills are killing people, and no one seems to be doing anything about it!"

Throughout Addison's struggles with addiction, not one of the countless pills that he ingested over the years was prescribed to him. He absconded with an unlimited supply of opiates, benzodiazepines, and muscle relaxers from friends and acquaintances with the apparent ease of ordering a cheeseburger at McDonald's. How, one might ask, in our pretty little town, was a college kid able to gain access to such a steady flow of narcotics with such little effort? I soon found out.

It was the "pill mill." Strategically situated and cleverly disguised amongst mid to high-end retail stores, a vast array of local and national restaurant chains, and mega-churches, pill mills were popping up everywhere and multiplying like cancer cells. They were unregulated, unmonitored, and run strictly as businesses for profit rather than healthcare establishments. For a flat cash fee of three to four hundred dollars, a patron could acquire his very own handpicked, deadly prescription cocktail.

To be candid, I never appreciated the magnitude of what was happening in my own backyard. My family had always assumed that Addison's death, and the deaths of his friends, were isolated incidents of good kids getting mixed up with the wrong crowd and making life-altering, ultimately life-ending mistakes. The individual family traumas were so devastating they were unmentionable; thus, no one talked about the overarching situation, so how were we to know Addison was one of hundreds of thousands? In reality, a plague had crept quietly into our community. It had traveled up Interstate 40 from our neighbors just south of us and settled in the heart of my world.

I first became aware of the *pain clinic epidemic*, as I like to call it, from a random news broadcast and from reading an article on the internet. Still, I couldn't believe this problem was in our pretty little city. Both journalistic pieces discussed Broward County, Florida. That's where all the news was happening because that area birthed the pain management clinics and had thrust itself onto the top of the podium, winning the number one spot in the country for prescription drug addiction and overdose deaths.

Leery of the liability of prescribing the evermore addicting and many times fatal narcotics, primary care physicians had begun to shy away from long-term pain management in their practices, which gave way to the all-encompassing *pain clinics*. Though the inception may have been rooted in good intentions—to help those fighting chronic back pain from a severe car accident or the patient suffering from the debilitating effects of multiple sclerosis— it took only a minute for someone to realize that there could be big business in the management of pain. The business that didn't treat patients but sought after customers proved to be extremely lucrative and deadly.

When Floridians finally realized the calamity that had befallen The Sunshine State, legislative action was taken. Bills were introduced, passed, and signed into law in an attempt to gain some control over the flood of legal poison being prescribed and sold illegally on seemingly every street corner throughout the state. In Florida pain clinics faced new rules that regulated all offices, including those with less-than-ethical intentions. State medical associations monitored prescriptions and provided oversight of doctors. Also, a mandated statewide database was created to curb doctor-shopping and prescription fraud. The primary legislative efforts in Florida seemed to be highly successful; however, the epidemic in Broward County did not end. It simply moved to Tennessee. The pain clinics found a cozy little home in our unregulated state. Seemingly overnight, they emerged and began their quiet destruction, and even families like my own, who were being directly affected by their arrival were taken completely by surprise.

Loving an addict lends itself to living in a bubble. Your world is focused inward, and your time, energy, and attention are allocated toward doing anything and everything you can to help the person you love. You tend to ignore communal and societal issues going on around you because your goal has become simplistic in nature. *Keep him alive and do whatever it takes to ensure his survival* becomes your mantra and daily existence. We tried everything in our power to do just that, but our attempts failed. God had plans for us, though.

It had been one week since Addison's death. Only two things that I knew for certain were that there was a hole in my heart that would remain for as long as it was beating, and that someone had to do something, and do it fast. I couldn't tolerate the idea that any sister, brother, parent, or friend would have to endure the pain I felt over losing Addison. I rapidly, almost instinctively, decided that I was going to do something. I was going to make sure fewer families had to suffer our kind of loss.

Though I didn't realize it at the time, I became like David. David was young, small, seemingly insignificant, but to defeat Goliath, he was chosen. I was just a sister, one citizen with no governmental experience, but I now know that I, too, was chosen. There is no other explanation for what happened next.

somebody help me

It's actually embarrassing to admit just how little I knew about government and legislation at the age of 32, despite my education. I needed help yet had little to no inclination as to where to begin. I was frenzied and very much in shock while fueled by a power from deep within. I didn't even stop to pray. I would like to say that I sat down and asked God for guidance on what to do and whom to call, but, of course, God knew exactly what and whom I needed without my having to ask.

Still seated in the kitchen with my mother on that cold January morning, I asked, "Maybe George Wallace can help me?"

"Maybe," she responded. "Call Mimi, I guess."

For many years my grandmother had worked for Caldwell Banker, Wallace & Wallace, a local real estate agency owned in part by Mr. George Wallace, who was also a local city councilman. I raced to their office within minutes of receiving the phone call that not only was Mr. Wallace willing and able to meet with me, but he was also immediately available. Willing to forego anything for this opportunity, I exploded into Mr. Wallace's conference room still clad in my pajamas. My hair was frizzed into oblivion, so I had quickly tied it on top of my head in a messy, tangled bun. With no makeup, the deep, black circles under my hollowed eyes exposed my grief for all the world to see.

I had always thought that Mr. Wallace was a rather attractive man with his dark features and tall, slender build, and he was a very sharp dresser. He had his own style, which included his colorful little bow ties, suspenders, and seersucker suits. Not many men can pull off that look as skillfully as he did. Though I had met Mr. Wallace several times on previous occasions, one would suspect that the mere sight of me on this particular day would elicit a reaction on his part, but he is a kind man and didn't bat an eye at my un-bathed, tousled appearance. He looked at me with sympathetic eyes as he offered his condolences and pulled out a chair for me.

Our meeting was brief, and though I have only vague memories of what was actually said, I do know that my speech and the presentation of my pleas were on par with my appearance. I spoke in frantic fragments, rattling off in rapid fire what little statistics I was aware of because my mouth was incapable of keeping up with my brain. I am certain, however, that I was proficient in expressing the desperation of our city's predicament and the very lives that hung in the balance unless someone did something, and did something quickly, as I exclaimed, "I just need somebody to help me!" After persuading me to stop and take a breath, Mr. Wallace advised me to call newly elected Senator Becky Duncan-Massey. He assured me that he would also place a call to her on my behalf, which he did that very afternoon. He also sent me an email.

January 9, 2012 @ 4:09PM

Jessica,

It was nice to meet with you today. As we discussed, I spoke with Becky Duncan Massey this afternoon about your concern of too many untimely deaths in Tennessee due to an overdose of prescription meds. I told her briefly about Addison and the horror surrounding those affected by this addiction. Becky is a lover of people and is also concerned about this problem.

Becky says that Ken Yeager, State Senator from Roane County, is pushing additional legislation through in attempt to curtail the distribution of prescription meds. She said she would speak with him this afternoon. I do not have his contact information, but I'm sure it's on the state website.

I have attached the regional legislative delegation directory. They are in session and working in Nashville Monday-Friday. Use each of their contact information to reach out to them. I will see many of them over the next couple of weeks and will remind them about this issue. Anything that comes up in local politics about pain clinics, I will fight against them.

Please keep me posted of your progress and let me know how I can help. May God bless you in this endeavor. Again, I'm sorry for your loss. I plan to speak with the Knoxville Police Chief about what can be done on the local level. I recognize that the illegal distribution of prescription meds is becoming an epidemic in our community.

I appreciate you bringing this to my attention.

Stay strong and keep the fight! I'm proud of you.
George C. Wallace
Broker/Owner Coldwell Banker Wallace & Wallace, Realtors
Knoxville, Tennessee

The email from Mr. Wallace was waiting on me when I arrived home and prepared to begin making phone calls. With both an office and cell phone number in hand, I nervously sat down to call this woman, this senator, whom I had never met, to ask for her help.

I knew that Senator Becky Duncan-Massey's brother, United States Congressman John J. Duncan Jr., lived just down the street from my parents, and that I had gone to middle school with his daughter. Other than that, I knew very little. I had never before called a senator and was unsure what to expect. Would she answer? If she answered, would she brush me off because I was a nobody calling her out of the blue? Would I have to leave a message with a receptionist or record a voicemail that had the possibility of going indefinitely unanswered?

I was pleasantly surprised at the kindness and warmth that greeted me during my first conversation with Becky, which I would later discover, took place on her very first day in office. She was reassuring and compassionate, and following her promise to guide and assist me, she gave me some immediate advice. She told me to contact Karen Pershing of the Knoxville Metropolitan Drug Commission and to start a Facebook page to raise awareness, and she informed me of another individual that I should call upon. "I will be in contact this afternoon with Senator Ken Yager," she said. "He is the one who sponsored the state-wide prescription database legislation, much like what they did in Florida. He is also sponsoring further pain clinic legislation this year. I will tell him about you and tell him to be looking for an email from you. He will be a lot of help to us." She explained to me about the pain clinic bill that he was currently sponsoring (Senate Bill 1258) and how to look it up on the state website so that I could read the proposed legislation, *myself*. She also advised me to pick a photograph of Addison and me and include it in every email that I sent. I chose my favorite picture of us and thought it only appropriate to also use it on the cover of this book.

Along with the thank you letter that I sent to Mr. Wallace, my first official email was to the man himself, the governor. I had gone to high school with Governor Bill Haslam's nieces, though, of course, I had never personally met him. I didn't expect much; after all, would the governor really read my message and write me back? Whether or not he wrote it himself, which is doubtful, I will never know, but I was pleased to get such a quick response. I followed his email with others to Senator Ken Yager and Karen Pershing of the Metropolitan Drug Commission as I was instructed. I was surprised by the immediate responses I received from everyone and by their willingness to help. God's provision amazed me as my path grew harder and longer as I continued. I trusted Him to see me through the human labor of what appeared to be a supernatural feat.

January 9, 2012 @ 3:49 PM

Dearest Governor Haslam,
My name is Jessica Akhrass (formerly Jessica Sharp). I went to Webb with Whitney and Cynthia and was in Whitney's graduating class of 1997. My brother Addison struggled with pain pill addiction for the past four years. My parents sent him to Capstone, which is a Christian-based rehab facility in Arkansas, for almost five months in 2009. His addiction only became worse upon his return, and his drug of choice escalated from Xanax to Roxicet and everything in between. He had been clean for about six months, making excellent grades at UT last semester, gaining almost 40 pounds, and passing random drug tests regularly.

We spend our Christmases in Nassau, which has been our family tradition for my entire life. We went this year and had a wonderful trip. I spent an amazing week with my baby brother and the rest of my family. He spoke with my parents Sunday night about how he was going to attend Bible Study Fellowship with my father. Every member of my family, including myself and my husband, has been a discussion leader for many years. He talked about his future plans and how he was so heartbroken for the pain he has caused us. For the thousands of dollars he stole to buy pills. For the sleepless nights and constant fear for his safety. He meant every word of what he said.

He wanted my mother to wake him in the morning to go to the vet to pick up his dog that he got at rehab because they did canine therapy there. When she went to wake him in the morning, she found him cold, already dead in his recliner. He had money left over from our trip and apparently had decided he was going to have one last hoorah before he turned his life around. His one more time WAS his last time.

We all searched his room to no avail, but his best friend found the pills the next day in his room. But what he found wasn't Roxicet. It was a horrible drug called Opana. This concoction is half morphine and half OxyContin. He somehow got his hands on the Extended Release form which is for hospice patients and is so potent that it is to be taken very specifically and should last over a twelve-hour period for patients in severe pain. The directions for this pill state that is should NEVER be crushed or broken, nor swallowed if the coating had been chipped because of the time release. As a drug user, Addison always crushed and snorted his pills. When he did this with this particular drug he received all twelve hours' worth of that much pain medication all at one time, which caused respiratory depression and ultimately his death.

I am writing to you in absolute DESPERATION for your help. I am so restless I just thought I would write to you as well as the other members of our state legislature that I have been in contact with. I need help, Governor.

We are so devastated from this loss. I was closer to my brother than any sister could be. I fought for him for years. I threatened drug dealers; I fought them tooth and nail to stay away from him. I couldn't begin to tell you what we have been through to save his life. Ultimately, he could not fight his addiction anymore, and the Lord welcomed him home. I am happy he isn't fighting this battle anymore, and I am confident as to where he is right now. He was strong in his faith, and he loved the Lord, but his demons were bigger than his human will.

The pain pill clinics in Knoxville and the surrounding areas are out of control. I don't know how all of these affluent, educated kids in their early twenties are getting such access to such deadly medication.

I need to meet with you. SOMETHING has to be done. Addison is the 4th of his friends to die from pain pill overdoses in the last three years, and that is just OUR family. For the people in Knoxville and the surrounding areas that have kids, siblings, and friends who have died in the recent past or are addicted to prescription drugs currently, I am begging for your help.

I knew if I needed to get something done, that I had to reach HIGH, which is why I am contacting you. Please respond to my message when you are available. I can't imagine how busy your schedule is, but no one can imagine the pain this has caused my family. It is unbearable, and I am realizing that our community as a whole is IGNORANT to the epidemic that we have going on right now.

This problem has exploded, and it is taking our youth, one young life at a time. I pray that you can help me legislatively in some way. I hope to hear from you soon by email or phone.
Sincerely,
Jessica Akhrass

January 11, 2012

Dear Friend,
Thank you for writing to me and sharing your concerns. I appreciate hearing from you.

After careful review of your letter, I have determined that the Tennessee Department of Health is the appropriate agency to address this type of inquiry, and therefore have forwarded your letter to Commissioner John J. Dreyzehner's office for consideration.

My administration is committed to providing effective and efficient service. If you have any further questions, please feel free to contact my office at 615-253-6913.

Again, thank you for taking the time to write. I look forward to working with you and all Tennesseans to make our great state an even better place to live, work, and raise a family.
Warmest regards,
Governor Bill Haslam

January 10, 2012 @ 1:07PM

Dearest Senator Yager,

My name is Jessica Akhrass. Senator Massey told me that she had spoken with you about me and my brother Addison. She told me that you would be in contact with me at some point, but I wanted to take this time to reach out to you and tell you a little more about my brother and express to you my deepest concerns about the problem we are facing in our community. We truly have an epidemic in our state with prescription pain medication. Our youth are dying on a daily basis, and the pain management clinics are playing a HUGE role in this matter.

My brother passed away eight days ago after fighting a pain pill addiction for four years. He was sent to Capstone, which is a Christian based rehab facility in Arkansas in 2009 for almost five months. His addiction only became worse once he returned home. He had experimented with every drug from Xanax to Roxicet and everything in between. Once he got addicted to opiates it was torture to watch him struggle, steal money from my parents, and do crazy irrational things that he would NEVER have done before. Our family doctor told us that once you are addicted to opiates, it changes your brain chemistry and your dopamine receptors so severely that even if you never took them again, the craving for that type of pill would stay with you for the rest of your life.

The coroner called my mother the other day to ask a question and told her that he had performed close to 1000 autopsies in Knox County and the surrounding areas in the last year, and that over HALF of them were kids under the age of 25 that had passed away from drug overdoses, and the majority of them were from pain medication. That number is STAGGERING. When I was in college at UT ten years ago, this was not an issue. I never knew anyone who took pain pills or died from an overdose from taking them. This problem has exploded, and it is taking our youth one young life at a time. Addison is the fourth of his friends to die in the last three years due to a drug overdose.
Here are my questions and concerns. I have read and reread the

summary of Bill 1258 regarding pain clinics. I realize that we can't just go and "shut them all down" and that there is a process that we must take to make changes. If you drive into a pain clinic parking lot you will see license plates from Georgia, North Carolina, and Alabama, to name a few. People are coming from other states to obtain literally HUNDREDS of pain pills to transport them across state lines. My questions are: How did this even get started? If citizens from other states are coming here to get these drugs, then obviously their states don't have the same problems as Tennessee. Why can't we do whatever it is that they are doing to eradicate this enormous issue?

What we have going on here in regard to the pain clinics (if you put it into the simplest of terms) is "legalized drug dealing." People who aren't even addicted to pain pills are frequenting the clinics to obtain medication for two to three dollars a pill and turning right around and selling them on the street for 30 - 40 dollars each. They are turning it into a business! A business that is killing HUNDREDS each year. I have many other questions and concerns and hope that I will get to meet with you at some point. I will do anything that you need me to do to assist in this matter. Senator Massey had mentioned the possibility of me coming to Nashville to testify for this bill. Please just tell me when and where, and I will be there. You have my full support, along with support from all of my family and friends in this matter.

Here are a few things I want people to know about my brother. He was so much more than just an addict. He was a highly intelligent, hilariously funny, and sensitive young man. We grew up in a Christian family, and he attended private Christian schools his entire life, as did I. He loved the Lord and had a strong foundation and faith in Christ. I know without a doubt where he is right now. If I didn't know that for sure, I don't know how I would deal with this tragedy.

Addison was so sweet, and loving, and kind. When his addiction took over, he became someone I didn't know and did things that we would never expect. I would see a glimpse of what I would call "the old Addison" from time to time, and it would make me happy. I did, however, along with my parents and husband, FIGHT for him for four solid years, enduring sleepless nights, being terrified when the phone rang at odd hours, and fighting off drug dealers face to face by myself (who, by the way, are kids Addison's age). I kept track of his phone while he was in rehab and did my own detective work when he got texts. I tried to crack their codes of "drug lingo" and tried to figure out who they were.

This truly has been a battle, and though nothing will bring my baby brother back, I will continue to fight by doing anything I can to help, but most importantly, Addison fought a huge battle, too. He tried so hard to stay away from pills. His friends said they had seen him turn them down dozens of times in an attempt to get clean. That is one of the reasons why his death was so shocking. We had arrived home from our annual Christmas vacation in the Bahamas, and he had been clean for six solid months. He was happy, he was making plans to go back to Bible Study Fellowship with my father, he had made good grades at UT last semester, and he had declared his major in psychology. I finally let go of the fear that I carried every day about his death, and the next morning my mother found him cold, having been gone for hours, lying in his recliner.

I am not ashamed of my brother. I am not embarrassed about him. I am proud of him for fighting the good fight. The Lord knew he couldn't fight it anymore and took him Home. After all that I have done for him over his entire life, especially over the last several years, this is something that he can now give to me. He is giving me a chance to help in the process of doing something that is important. He has given me a purpose to be able in some way to help other families so they will not have to go through what we are experiencing right now. The void I feel without Addison sometimes seems unbearable but knowing that through his death I could possibly help in making a difference is the best gift he could have ever given me, and I will be grateful for that forever. I hope to hear from you soon. I would love to meet with you, and I will do whatever it takes to help. Enclosed is my favorite picture of Addison and me. It is from Thanksgiving of last year. You can tell

from the photograph that he was loved. I don't want him to be just a statistic. He was a person. He was my brother, whom I loved more than anything. We were two peas in a pod though there were ten years between us.
Sincerely,
Jessica Akhrass
January 10, 2012 @ 3:15 PM

Jessica,
Thanks for your email. I really appreciate your support, although it must be so painful for you. What a loss. I plan to respond in more detail to your thoughtful letter but just wanted to acknowledge it today, and Becky has talked to me about you, too.
Sen Yager

January 13, 2012 @ 4:10 PM

Jessica,
Thank you so much for sharing your passion and the story of your brother so freely with me. I have been in my job for only a year and a half and have been doing what I can to wake people up to the issue and the fact that we can no longer afford to sit back. We need to take bold actions. It is very difficult when processes don't move as quickly as we'd like for them to.

I have been working with local legislators and know that they are committed to seeing things change, as is Governor Haslam. You are right in that we have to recognize that there are people who are truly in pain and need the assistance that these medications can provide.

I am working with physicians and hospitals to implement screening tools to identify early signs of addiction and hopefully intervene before a person's brain chemistry has been forever altered. We have to get the medical community behind resolving this problem and helping to alleviate it. We have to always be mindful that this epidemic didn't happen overnight, and the solutions to reverse the trend will also take time to put in place and implement. That certainly does not bring your brother or his friends back or others that may perish in the meantime. It grieves me knowing that time is ticking and for some the clock will stop before we can reach them.

I would love to have the privilege to meet you and talk to you. You have a very powerful story that you are obviously more than willing to share. Maybe we can come up with some creative ways to pool our resources and make a difference today.

I cannot tell you how sorry I am for the loss of your brother, but I know you will use this experience to help MANY others. You already are.

Please let me know when you might be available to meet.
Respectfully,
Karen

Karen Pershing, MPH
Executive Director
Metropolitan Drug Commission
4930 Lyons View Pike
Knoxville, Tennessee 37919

I met with Karen Pershing the following week. I don't remember much of what we said, but I felt an immediate connection with her from the very beginning when she shared with me the loss of her sister to an automobile accident many years ago. She understood the pain of losing a sibling. She "got" me. We talked over coffee, and I do remember her telling me that she didn't quite understand how I was sitting in front of her and was prepared to take on such a gargantuan task just two weeks after Addison's death. "God," I said. He was my only explanation of how I could be there so soon. By all other accounts there is no possible way that I could have begun such a journey so quickly.

As I reread those first emails and the subsequent responses, I am reminded, however vaguely, of how desperate and feverish I was during that time. I couldn't let overdoses keep happening to so many others. My messages were long and free-flowing, and many of the sentences were just fragmented thoughts. I can remember not taking very much time to think about how they were written. I had so much to say and at that point was mentally incapable of condensing. I would sit down with the laptop and my fingers would begin to fly. Many times, I would polish off a message and send it without even reading it first though over the next eighteen months, as the shock began to wear off and my senses began to return to me, I was able to better articulate myself though often my letters and emails still read as giant rants full of urgency, desperation, and anger.

I must have written ten thousand emails, maybe more. I began with the senators; there were 33 of them in Tennessee, a fact that I embarrassingly had not known. I then moved on to the state representatives, there were 99, another fact that I was clueless about. I sent each and every one of them a message very similar to those that I had sent to Senator Yager and Governor Haslam in my very first days of work. I announced to them who I was, and I explained to them my mission. I asked for their help and reiterated the desperation of our current situation. I told them about Addison and who he was as a person. I told them all of the wonderful and good things about him and how much he was loved. I assured them that they would hear from me again, and often, and I began to sign my letters with:

Sincerely,
Addison's Sister

A.D.D.I.S.O.N.

Within a few hours of curling up in my bed with a pen and a sheet of paper, I had come up with a name for my Community Facebook page that Senator Massey had instructed me to create. Throughout my journey from the very beginning it was extremely important to me that Addison was remembered. In the months that followed and the thousands of people that I communicated with, I could care less if they remembered my name, just as long as they didn't forget his. With this in mind I named the Facebook page after him calling it, "A.D.D.I.S.O.N." (*Abolish Drug Distribution Igniting Support of New-Beginnings*).

    The mission statement for my page was to honor my baby brother, to raise awareness, to unite in support against the unethical practices of the pain clinics that were killing our citizens, and to join me in the legislative fight to prevent future tragedies. But almost immediately it became so much more than that. Not long after my first few posts of introducing myself, explaining the intent of my page, and giving my vow to create the laws necessary to stop the hemorrhage in our great state, the Facebook page exploded. It was viewed nearly half a million times and liked by thousands within a few short months.

It wasn't until the dozens upon dozens of daily messages began pouring in that I started to realize the magnitude of what we were facing. I had placed very strict rules on my page, making it clear to everyone that it was a "safe place" for people to communicate and share their experiences free from judgment. I did not tolerate arguing, shaming, or degradation of any kind and was prudent at monitoring the activity on the page to ensure that my new group of friends felt secure.

I never ceased in my posts of stressing that addiction is a DISEASE. I tried to rally the supporters in standing up for themselves and those that they love who battle the disease or who have died trying. I told them NOT to be embarrassed, that they were more than just addicts; they were people, kind people, smart people, funny people, just like my brother. I urged them not to allow themselves or their family members and friends to become defined by their disease, and I told them that I understood their struggle and their pain in the only way that I could, as a sister who had watched her brother struggle to death.

I promised them that I would get something done to save more people from dying or being forced to live without someone they love for the rest of their lives. At this point I had no idea what that "something" would be. I didn't begin with a list of laws that I wanted to pass; God had not revealed them to me yet, but I tried to empower people and support them, and with only my vague promise of help, they latched onto me, some of them for dear life.

For the next eighteen months, I became like Dear Abby, and I soon began to realize that I was giving an entire cross section of society something that they had never had before, a place where fear of embarrassment, guilt, and shame didn't exist. Of the thousands of messages that I received such a vast majority of them were talking about their addiction or the addiction of a loved one for the very first time, to me, a total stranger.

Dear Jessica,
I just wanted to say that I think it is absolutely amazing what you are doing. I lost my brother four years ago to a continuous battle with prescription drugs and never had the courage to speak out against it. In fact, my family never talks about it at all. I am always afraid that people will place judgment upon my brother and he would not be able to stand up for himself. My brother was 23 when he passed away. If there is anything I can do to help spread the word please let me know. Seeing you stepping up and speaking out really hit home to me. These pain clinics are like the plague, and I would give anything to have had the courage to take a stand when the plague struck my family. Thank you for taking a stand. Let me know if there is anything I can do to help. God Bless you and your family.
Sincerely,
H.M.

Jessica,
You are such a blessing from GOD!!! I've lost several people I know due to a pill OD. I know countless people where I live, in Tennessee, that are addicted to pills. It hurts my heart to watch how it changes their lives. My husband has been fighting addiction for four years now. I don't speak about it to anyone. We have an 11-year-old son, and GOD love him, he has been through more than any child his age should have to. I have about lost my husband many times, and I pray a lot! He has cleaned up, and I still worry each day that he might slip up. I pray to GOD that this pill epidemic will be brought down. I work at a pharmacy and see how many of different milligrams of 3-4 different pain meds one doctor will give to one patient. One person gets 200+ strength of Oxy, 200+ strength of Roxy, Xanax, and Soma! In all, she probably walks out with over 800 pain pills each month. It blows my mind that the doctors can write that many pills for one person. There should be a

limit on how many pills a doctor can write to one person. I am so against pain pills and pill mills. They about destroyed my life! I am SO glad you are working on this. It's such a sad thing, and I'm so sorry you lost Addison to addiction. Like you said, GOD is using you and him. You're an angel. God bless you and your family in your healing, fighting for this cause, and thank you for this fb page. You are such an inspiration!
K.F.

Jessica,
First off, I am so sorry you lost your brother, it's clear you were very close. My name is C.C., I am a sergeant in the US Army, I am 27 years old, I am married, and my wife and I have a daughter on the way. I am also addicted to pain pills. I first tried OxyContin when I was in high school right after my grandfather suddenly passed away. I had no idea what I was getting myself into, or the impact that it would have on my life. On summer break between my junior and senior year, I met one of my friend's parents who was happy to sell me his OxyContin. I missed half of my senior year as a result, lost my scholarship to Duke, and my future. I coasted by for several years and then moved to Fort Myers Florida. I eventually developed a habit that required about ten 80mg pills a day, which the pill mill doctors were more than happy to supply. I lived this way for about five years until Florida finally started to regulate the distribution of pills.

In late 2008 I decided to it was time to do something with my life. I was desperate to break the hold that pills had on me. I enlisted in the US Army to try and get my life back. Boot camp was the worst time of my life, and withdrawal was hell. Withdrawal with a drill sergeant is a whole new level of hell.

I graduated boot camp in May of 2009, and my first duty station was at Fort Hood, TX, but I took a leave in between boot camp and going to Fort Hood because I could not stay sober. I came back to Knoxville and bought pills that night, it was my first real time paying "street price" and I was stunned at how people could afford them every day. I was soon deployed to Afghanistan and while I was away, I lost six people that I was close to, and I took part in things of war that I will never forget. I was also struck by several IED's.

I returned home and married my high school sweetheart. She is also a pain pill addict. I have been clean for almost two years now, but it is a daily struggle to stay that way because the supply seems endless. I cannot speak to my old friends, and I cannot go to Florida or anywhere near Knoxville. I have to keep a distance from the temptation that is so great in those places.

If there is anything that I can do to help you change the laws, I would be happy to do so. I admire your determination, your courage, and your resolve. We have got to regulate these doctors and clinics. Currently, the demand is unquenchable, the profit incalculable, and as long as there is money to be made there will be people willing to dispense completely unnecessary amounts of pills, knowing they are killing people. Please let me know what I can do to help.
US ARMY Sergeant C.C.

I was astounded at the sheer volume of outcry from so many people. I began each morning at the crack of dawn reading message after message, and my heart broke as I absorbed their pain and relived my own. I sobbed as I lay in my pajamas, typically wrapped in a blanket on my olive-green couch, reading for hours and then subsequently writing back to each and every one of them. My entire body ached for them as they poured out their stories, their secrets, to someone they had never met. They were desperate and saw me as a light in a world that had turned so dark. To this day I don't understand the notion of people calling me an inspiration, which is something that over time I began to hear on more occasions than I can count. I had a sergeant in the United Stated Army, a man who had been to WAR, telling me that I was courageous. ME? I didn't feel courageous; I felt heartbroken and angry at the injustice and just did what I thought was right. Having never been someone who struggled with transparency, I had no problem exposing every horrible truth about my own experience to the world, and as it turned out the transparency began to catch on.

After filling an entire album on Facebook entitled "Remembering Addison" containing pictures of our family that spanned the entirety of his life, I decided to create "Loved Ones Lost," which was a space on our page to honor others and was dedicated to the memory of loved ones we have lost to the disease of addiction. I invited people to post their family members' photographs to allow them to be more than statistics, to show their faces, and to show that they were loved.

I also created a Prayer Request album, which contained written Prayer Requests and photographs of those currently struggling with addiction. The list was not only shared countless times across the internet, but also people began printing them out and sharing them with their church groups. This album was particularly heartbreaking because many times I was sent photographs of people who were not only known addicts, but also missing. I received pictures of people who had been incarcerated for drug-related charges, young teenagers whose parents were seeking prayer, photos of infants born addicted to prescription pills and taken from their mothers to spend the first two months of their lives in detox, and even a couple of ultrasound photos of unborn children who had addicted parents.

There were so many people in so much pain, like I was, and in an instant, I had bonded with them. Countless of them had already endured such a catastrophic loss and were there to encourage me. I poured my heart out in daily posts, about everything. I told these people how long it had been since I had last eaten or taken a shower, how many cigarettes I had smoked, how many times I had lain in the floor and cried the day before, and every single memory that popped into my head about Addison. They lifted me up through reassuring words and countless prayers, and I came to depend on them as much as they counted on me. Late into the night or the wee hours of the morning when I was exhausted and felt confused as to why I had even begun and had no idea what step I should take next, God would send someone my way with a message to keep me going.

Dearest Jessica,
I love you. We don't even know each other, but I FEEL like you must be my sister. I cannot begin to tell you how great what you are doing is and how many LIVES are and will be saved when you are finished. This epidemic has always lacked a voice, and yours is being heard loud and clear. Not to mention you are recruiting additional voices so as to ensure the maximum volume.

I am A.A.M., and I was addicted to prescription pills (OxyContin) and Heroin for six years. I have been clean for a little over three years. I should be dead 100 times over, but I am not by the Grace of God. Because God made beauty from my ashes, I am able to carry my message of hope to those that suffer and hurt. For the longest time, I believed "once an addict, always an addict." THAT IS NOT WHO I AM!!! It's what I was choosing to do, but not who I was. Anyhoo, that is enough about me. I just want you to know that I pretty much stalk the page (lol), LOVE what you are doing and am in awe of your strength. You choose to draw on the strength of our Heavenly Father, and boy oh boy, He is going to use you in a mighty way! If there is ever anything specifically I can do to help you in any way, please let me know. I pray

for you and your family daily. I wish I could have known Addison. He sounds like an absolutely lovely and enjoyable person.
Much Love to You,
A.A.M.

It sounds crazy, but we became a giant family of struggling people who had never met, bound together in a club that no one would ever want to be a member of. I loved them, and I cared for them deeply. They shared things with me that they hadn't shared with another living soul. They felt a connection to me and I to them. Shortly after creating the A.D.D.I.S.O.N. page, my personal Facebook page began to light up with friend requests of people I had been messaging. Having met exactly NONE of them, I was very careful as to whom I let in to my private account because you never know whom you are actually talking to on the internet. There were a dozen or so, however, that I did let in and we have become very good friends, and a small handful that really did become family. God handpicked a select few. They became like a mother, a brother, and the sister I never had. They are people I treasure and people whom, had I not endured this tragedy, I would have never known.

steph, matt & sandy

Of the thousands of people that I began to regularly communicate with there was a small group that I became especially attached to, but none so much as Stephanie, Matt, and Sandy. Though, of course, no one could ever take Addison's place, through his loss God provided me with three strangers I grew to love like my own family. God led each of them to Addison's Facebook page, and we bonded quickly following their very first messages.

Steph was in her early twenties when she lost her own brother to the disease of addiction. Though the circumstances surrounding their deaths were dissimilar, he seemed to have so much in common with Addison. Young, bright, handsome, he came from a nice family who lived just a fifteen-minute drive from where Addison and I grew up. Like Addison he had the world at his fingertips. He died at the youthful age of 24. His photographs portray him just as Steph always described, with his kind eyes and gentle smile. Like my own brother, no one would have ever suspected from looking at him the demons that he battled, and Steph's family was just as shocked as my own that he would end up in combat against this disease.

While I was communicating with countless others who, unfortunately, understood the agony of losing a sibling,

Steph became a source of compassion and encouragement for me in a way that only the Lord could understand and provide through another human being. We were simpatico despite the fact that she is so unlike me. I always describe her as sugar and spice and everything nice; that's Steph. Whereas, I am bold, loud, and opinionated, Steph is sweet, and mild. Those traits typically annoy me, but she is genuine, and it shows. She lost her brother several years before Addison's death and would be the first to remind me that the pain would not kill me. We would stay up late into the night messaging back and forth. She cried with me, prayed for me, and was always sending sweet gifts in the mail from simple little greeting cards that she happened to find to books on grief and how to let the word of God sustain me. She became my fast friend to this day and is the sister I never had.

Like Steph and her brother, Matt grew up just a short drive from our family home in neighboring Oak Ridge. In all of my life, I have never met another person who reminded me so much of my Addison, and I saw it from the moment he happened upon Addison's Facebook page. He's a smartass, and his sarcastic yet endearing wit never disappoints when I need a good laugh. Charming and charismatic, Matt is audacious yet kind and sincere. He is also an addict, and what began with prescription pills eventually led to an appetite for heroin. Matt is another example. He has a healthy family background, and he is college-educated. No one would suspect he is an addict. No one would guess he has been arrested, has spent time behind bars, and has injected himself in the neck to get high. But, like I reiterated to everyone on Addison's Facebook page and hope that Matt continues to remember, those are just things he has done. They are not who he is.

We talked frequently on the internet, messaging back and forth about his struggles and my grief. He listened to my pain and attempted to give me insight from Addison's perspective, which I found very comforting. He also provided me with valuable information regarding pills and the epidemic on the streets that I would later use for our cause. Before I had an opportunity to block them, Matt was always the first to come to my defense when haters appeared on Addison's page with verbal attacks against Addison or when an "internet troll" (as Matt calls them) personally attacked me on media websites because they claimed that my mission was to "take everyone's pain medication away," and they often accused, "You are making other people suffer because your brother was an idiot."

Though the struggle continues, and he has had a few relapses, I am happy to say that Matt is currently in recovery. I pray daily that his path will become easier and thank God that He allows me to walk alongside Matt through his journey. Addison never wanted to burden us with his difficulties, and I have learned that Matt struggles with this as well, but he has given me an opportunity that Addison so often shut me out of because he didn't want me to worry. Just a simple text to let me know how his day is going is a gift. While we continue to talk regularly, my only regret is that I still have not met him, my friend whom I have grown to call my brother, in person, a fact that I hope to remedy someday soon.

I will never forget the day I met Sandy. It was June 4, 2012, almost five months to the day since Addison had gone to be with the Lord. After coming across Addison's Facebook page and offering an enormous amount of prayer, Sandy sent me a private message and requested to meet me. With the amount of attention I had been receiving from my legislative efforts, her request did not seem odd at the time, and upon discovering that she was also one of my husband's dental patients, I invited her over. It was early afternoon when her white Lexus pulled into my driveway. I noticed as the blue-eyed, platinum blonde emerged from her car and approached my front porch that she seemed to be around the same age as my mother, and in her late fifties, maybe. She carried with her several sheets of paper and a small heart-shaped box made of tin. Her kindness was obvious from the very beginning. She was soft spoken, and at first, I detected a small degree of apprehension.

I couldn't blame her. I would be slightly nervous, too, if I had shown up at a total stranger's house and told her that God had sent me there as an encourager. She handed me a letter, which she had received while working among the rubble and devastation at Ground Zero following the 9/11 attacks during her time with The American Red Cross. I noticed immediately that the letter was dated October 26, my birthday. The letter began with "Dear Miracle Makers," and it continued on as a thank you letter from a widow, whose husband had been tragically lost in the attack on the World Trade Center, but whose wedding ring had been miraculously found and returned to her. Sandy gave me a copy of this letter and explained to me that I, too, was a Miracle Maker.

Inside the heart-shaped box was a mustard seed encased in a translucent, amber colored rock. "All you have to have is the faith of a mustard seed, and you can move mountains," she said. She assured me that Addison's law would be successful, that I was going to make a difference, that there was a grand and unique calling upon my life, and that God had sent her to help, support, and encourage me.

There was something odd about this woman. She was so calming with her mannerisms, the gentleness of her voice, the steady and measured way in which she spoke; she was opposite of my extroverted confidence, which many times allows whatever I am thinking to escape my lips without pause.

I was born to the most wonderful woman in the world, who also happened to be wound tighter than an eight-day clock; therefore, this consistent tranquility appeared foreign. I knew at that moment that I had never met anyone like her and am confident now that I never will. The love of Jesus seemed to ooze from her very being. I loved her almost immediately and could never have comprehended how important she would become in my life.

We talked for hours, perched on my front porch on that warm June afternoon. I eventually led her around back to show her my willow trees. Addison and I had planted them together three years prior when he returned home from a stay in rehab and right before my rib-crushing horseback riding accident that left me bedridden with Addison by my side for weeks. Though he hadn't let on, he was convinced that the little saplings would never survive, given the hard and rocky ground in which they were planted. "I don't have the heart to tell her," he told our mother, "that those trees are never gonna make it." Not only did they make it, but they also flourished, growing fast and large. They were enormous and beautiful, and I eventually found solace beneath them as I spent time under those willow trees talking to my brother and praying to the Lord.

Sandy is a Prayer Warrior. Anyone who knows her knows this. Though at our first meeting I was years away from even remotely beginning to understand the gravity, magnitude, and volume of this anointing and calling upon my life that she spoke of so confidently, my trust in her wisdom and guidance was immediate. I learned quickly that when Sandy told me that she was praying for me, she meant it, and that hers were fervent, faithful prayers of expectancy, a practice that she is still trying to teach me to master with consistency. I have learned so much from this woman, a woman I soon began to call my second mother, and a woman I simply could not imagine my life without.

What saddens me the most about these three incredibly special people and the thousands of people whom I met, connected with, and communicated with on a daily basis, is the fact that they never knew Addison. His life, struggles, and death surrounded so much of our conversations and so many of them never got to know how wonderful he was. Though I posted memories about him daily, and many people posted back that they loved hearing about him and felt as if they knew him, I always felt inadequate in describing how extraordinary he was and how much I loved him.

channel 6

My first of many news appearances was on the 6th of February in 2012. In the month since its inception, Addison's Facebook page and my vow to stop the death and destruction sweeping our state from the poison of prescription pills had spread like wildfire. The onslaught of requests from local reporters that followed was both exciting and overwhelming. Though I was eating, sleeping, and breathing my work, Addison had only been gone for a month, and I had just begun to really enter the throes of grief.

    I was taken aback when the phone rang at four o'clock in the afternoon and the person on the other end asked for an interview request, which he wanted to shoot in 30 minutes. Thirty MINUTES? He clearly had no comprehension of what I looked like still in my pajamas, having not showered in days. He wanted me camera ready in half an hour? It happened many more times. Each time, we had the same conversation. "You all are going to have to give me more notice than 30 minutes because there's no way in hell I can look even a little bit presentable in that amount of time!"

    Our first taping took place, of course, at my mother's house, not only because there weren't four extremely large dogs barking and wandering around like at my house, but also because my mother obviously wanted to be a part of the whole experience. I obliged because hers was Addison's and my home. It's also more spacious and prettier, and um, cleaner than mine. My face was flushed and my heart was racing when the cute little Asian reporter, Hana Kim, and her cameraman Steve rang the doorbell. Even after all my years of modeling and fashion shows and horse competitions, I was still a bit nervous about being on television for the first time. Hana's kind, compassionate demeanor reassured me, and I began to remind myself to muster that boldness that was usually so abundant.

After running microphone wires up the front of my sweater and stuffing a battery pack down into the back of my jeans, Hana and Steve checked the lighting and sound. I sat in one of my mother's black upholstered wingback chairs in front of the hearth that was covered in framed photographs of Addison (as Hana had requested). My mother sat behind the camera on the staircase in the foyer so that she could watch. Throughout the interview, which lasted nearly a half hour, I just kept thinking to myself, *How in the world are they going to edit this down to just a couple of minutes? I've said so much and what if they cut out the parts that I feel are the most important?* I expressed my concerns to Hana about the editing process and made clear to her things that I did not want removed, knowing damn good and well that once it was over that I was basically at their mercy and discretion. Once the story aired, I realized Hana's trustworthiness and reliability as a reporter, and thus became loyal to her in the future for my media outlet, knowing that she would honor my requests.

I posted on Addison's Facebook page the day before my story was going to air so that everyone could tune in. The "troops," as I lovingly began to call them, were bursting with excitement, as was my entire family as we set every DVR to record and huddled together in front of the flat screen in my parents' living room. As the newscast began and I realized that we were the top story of the night, my breath caught in my throat and my mother began to cry as we saw my favorite picture of Addison and me pop up on the huge screen. I heard the sound of my own voice. "The day that he died was, by far, the worst day of my life," I said.

I then saw myself seated in that black wingback chair and being interviewed as Hana voiced over, "Jessica Akhrass says her family did everything they could to save her little brother, Addison Sharp, from the poisonous addiction to prescription pills." They began to show still photographs of me and Addison that I had given them permission to gather from our Facebook page. "You know, my mom asked him about the first pill that he took, 'Did you even know what it was?' and he said, 'No.' So, it just started out that way and escalated from Xanax to Roxicet and beyond," I said.

Upon zooming in on the life-sized senior yearbook portrait of Addison that had stood at the front of the sanctuary at his funeral, Hana began the synopsis of our story, "The Catholic High School grad got hooked when he was eighteen. In 2009, the family says he overdosed on Xanax. Taking a break from classes at UT, Sharp went to an out of state, faith-based rehab center. Shortly before Addison's death, the family had just gotten back home from a vacation. They say Addison was in good spirits; after all, they say he was clean from prescription pills for about six months, and they finally thought that he had taken a turn for the better. Addison's mother found him dead last month in their Farragut home at the young age of 22."

"A friend of his found them, in a hiding place in his room that none of us would have ever thought to look. There was pill residue on the counter," I said.

Hana then stated, "The family is waiting for autopsy results to confirm their belief that Addison died of an overdose."

I said, "He talked to my parents and told them, 'The pills ate my soul; they made me do things that I would never have done.'"

Hana had clearly done her research when she began laying out statistics, "The CDC says prescription medication is the reason for the rise in drug overdose deaths in the country. The Southwest and Appalachian regions have the highest rates. Tennessee's Department of Health released the latest statistics on sixteen East Tennessee counties. Every SINGLE County except one reported an increase in accidental drug overdose deaths over the last several years. When we compare 2003 to 2010, here are the numbers: Knox County saw a 41 percent spike in overdose deaths. Look at these other counties. The spike is jaw dropping. For example, Blount and Roane Counties saw 107 percent and 125 percent increases while Hamblen County experienced a 160 percent increase and Sevier County a whopping 187.5 percent. We sat down with Roane County Sheriff Jack Stockton."

"If there's not some way to regulate and hold the persons responsible that are dishing out these pills from the pain clinics, then there's definitely going to be more issues and problems," Stockton said.

Hana stated, "Stockton fears the trend in overdose deaths will skyrocket; so does Akhrass."

The video switched back to a shot of me in that black chair sitting next to Addison's picture, "I don't want this to happen to anyone else. I know that the legislative system works slowly, and I'm afraid of how many more deaths of young people that will happen before those laws can be put into place."

"Akhrass plans to lobby lawmakers to work faster. If you ask Tennessee Lieutenant Governor Ron Ramsey, the epidemic is a priority. 'This is serious,' said Ramsey, 'and I think we as legislators understand that, and we're going to do all we can to correct it.'"

Hana began wrapping up her story with a picture of Addison and our parents on the beach in Nassau. It had been taken just a month earlier and was the last photograph of us as a whole family. "Addison's family is doing their part to protect their community by launching this Facebook page not only to remember Addison, but also to send one important message."

"It's a very hidden issue," I said. "It's hidden, and people NEED to talk about it and not be ashamed because their kids are highly educated, went to good schools, and come from good families. It's EVERYWHERE, and it's killing young people."

"Akhrass says three young men, all friends of her brother, also lost their lives to prescription pills, making Addison the fourth tragedy in this small community. In Farragut, Hana Kim, six News."

Only Addison wasn't just the fourth tragedy in our community. Our situation was far worse, a desperate condition. According to the Knox County Coroner, who had spoken to my mother personally on the phone, there had been over one thousand autopsies performed in our county alone in a matter of months, and over half of the dead were kids under the age of 25. Addison was one tragedy out of THOUSANDS of tragedies in just one year. It seemed like an entire generation of people were dying, and every single death was 100 percent preventable.

The Lieutenant Governor's comments during my news segment angered me, particularly when he said the situation was serious and that "legislators understood." Irate, I thought, *They don't understand anything! If they did, someone would have done something by now to stop this madness! They have no clue! Their statistics are so far off base you could use the paper they were printed on as toilet paper.* I guess my anger was misguided, and I shouldn't have been angry with the legislative body as a whole. How fortunate they were that this epidemic had not hit them in their own homes, with their own kids and loved ones. How could they understand if it had never directly affected them? Which made me think, *How is THAT possible?* The answer is, it's NOT.

If you walk up to anyone, and I mean anyone, anywhere, at any time, pretty much in any city in the state of Tennessee, and mention prescription pills, if the person is open and honest, he or she can tell you a personal story, or the story of a friend or an acquaintance, or the story of a fellow church member who is addicted, was addicted, arrested, overdosed, and/or died from prescription pills. You will hear how addiction has destroyed the addicts' lives and the lives of everyone around them. People see it in their jobs, in schools, on the streets, and, of course, in pain clinic parking lots overflowing with cars from surrounding counties and surrounding states. How could 33 senators and 99 state representatives be immune to the plague?

My realization of the answer to this question was so troubling to me, so disturbing, that it broke my heart and set a fire ablaze within my soul all at the same time. There was somebody, probably a handful, or maybe a dozen of somebodies who worked in that Legislative Plaza in Nashville who had more intimate knowledge of what was ravaging our state and our families than they cared to admit. My comprehension of this saddened me so deeply because, just as I had said in my news interview about the epidemic being a "hidden issue," it hit me that it's SO hidden that we as a community, as a society, as Tennesseans would rather sit back and let people die rather than be embarrassed. God forbid people admit that they or people they love are battling addiction! Lord no, they couldn't admit that! The idea of hiding in shame while we buried our citizens was unfathomable to me, and I was having no more of it. Not one more second.

I wanted to meet the sheriff whom Hana Kim interviewed for our news story. Sheriff Jack Stockton was not my sheriff in Loudon County, but of our neighboring Roane County, which is two counties over from Knox County. He was seated in his office during his part of the news interview. He wore a bright red sweater and sported a military style buzz cut. There was just something about the man.

God told me, "You need to meet him." I was drawn to Stockton and from the one sentence that they aired of his interview on the news you could just tell he was a kind man. He seemed soft spoken and even-tempered; there was a sadness and deep concern in his eyes as he spoke of the plight of our state's future if something wasn't done about the pill mills.

From one sentence I could tell that he deeply cared about this issue, and then I heard my nudge from the Lord. Within a week my mother and I were seated in that same sheriff's office that I had seen on TV when Jack Stockton was interviewed. Our meeting turned out to be powerful and moving, but the first thing among many things that Stockton did on the day that we met, was give me a new name.

erin brockovich

It was a matter of minutes into our conversation with Roane County Sheriff Jack Stockton when he politely interrupted me and asked, "Have you seen the movie, *Erin Brockovich*?" We exchanged confirming smiles. He laughed and knowingly wagged his finger at me, "Good because I've just got a feeling about you," he said. He looked at my mother, still smiling, and said, "This one is going to get something done here and maybe ruffle a lot of feathers doing it." We had just met and yet he had such immediate confidence in me. Strangely, I felt like "he got me." Though Sherriff Stockton was the first to compare me to the bold, brash, outspoken, tenacious yet inexperienced Erin Brockovich, he would not be the last. As time passed, it seemed to become a theme throughout law enforcement, in particular, that people called me *Erin*, a nickname that I rather liked. Her real life story became more and more of an inspiration to my own situation and our seemingly unrelated stories eventually had much more in common than I had ever dreamed.

Though featured with only his one-liner the night of my first news appearance, Channel 6 had interviewed Sherriff Stockton in depth on the following night for Part II of their six-part series on the prescription drug epidemic in Tennessee. It was his honesty and transparency that first drew me to Jack. His interview was less about his role as the Sheriff and more about how the epidemic was sweeping through our communities and affecting everyone, increasing crime, increasing incarcerations, and skyrocketing accidental overdose deaths. But his real message was about his own son Toby. Toby was just a few years younger than I, had grown up in a loving Christian home as the son of the County sheriff, but was currently being housed in the Fentress County Jail for his umpteenth drug possession arrest.

To hear Sheriff Stockton explain Toby's history during his television interview was much like listening to our own family story. He was a good kid, a smart kid, a loving and generous person. He was also addicted to prescription pills, and despite everyone's efforts just could not get clean and stay clean. I was proud of the sheriff's openness to talk about Toby on television without shame. He was disheartened, broken in a way, and sorrow filled his sympathetic eyes, but he was not ashamed, and that is what led me to his office.

I was pleasantly surprised that I was able to call his office, give a brief explanation of who I was, explain my agenda, and receive an open invitation for my mother and me the very next morning. Sherriff Stockton was warm and welcoming. We sat in his office for nearly an hour, swapping stories about Addison and Toby, and discussing the horrors of being the Sherriff trying to fight a losing battle while watching your community being ravaged. "Do you know how badly it breaks my heart to see kids that I taught in Sunday school locked up in my jail?" he asked. "Toby grew up with these kids. These kids played together. I know their families, and to see them now is . . . well, just heartbreaking," he said, shaking his head.

Sheriff Stockton made his point clearer by taking us through the jail. I had never been on a jail tour, and it was actually quite intimidating. As we were buzzed into each corridor through the thick steel doors, I couldn't help but notice the sterility of the stark white, barren hallways. The echoes of our shoes carried on forever. It was immaculately clean yet made me feel uncomfortable and germy, much like a hospital does. Jack explained historical facts to us regarding tiny Roane County and about the construction and jail house renovations, all of which were interesting at the time, and none of which I remember today. Mainly we talked about the overcrowding and the reason for the overcrowding, of course, was prescription pill arrests. Nearly 85 percent of the inmates at that time were incarcerated for prescription drug offenses, from possession, to prescription fraud, to driving under the influence. The sheer numbers of incarcerations were alarming, and the majority of them were re-arrests. Sadly, released offenders would return in just a short time.

I hesitated to look into the cell "pods" as they were called as we walked the long hallways, despite Jack's invitation to take a peek. Somehow staring in at the inmates through the small square window in the six-inch thick door was unnerving. The only thing I could think of was the animals on display at the zoo, caged animals. I felt that looking in on them would make them feel uncomfortable, like I was invading what miniscule amount of privacy they had left. Though I knew that each and every one of them had broken the law, that they had all done something to end up behind bars, I still felt a deep sense of compassion for them. I saw them as someone's son or daughter, someone's sister or brother, who could have very easily been my own relative. I saw them as sufferers from disease rather than criminals with ill intent. My heart broke for them because I knew, like Addison, that had it not been for the addiction to drugs, most of them would not have done whatever it was that they did to end up in jail.

Even Jack admitted that previously he had little to no compassion for people jailed for drug offenses. "They chose to do drugs, so it was their own fault. I didn't feel sorry for them at all," he said. "Until it was my own son, and I saw how he struggled, and I saw how he fought, and I knew what a good person he was, and I realized that his decision to do drugs boiled down to one bad and incredibly stupid choice that he made on one particular day of his life. God help us all if we were judged and condemned for life based on one bad and incredibly stupid decision. How many times have I made the wrong choice on any given day? Haven't we all?"

Jack led us up to the top floor and into a large open space with six to eight-foot square sections of the floor that were constructed of thick tempered glass. It took me only a second to realize that we were now standing above the cell pods. As we walked we saw inmates mulling around below in what no doubt was an incredibly boring existence. Far worse than boredom were the addicts that I witnessed below suffering through the throes of withdrawal. Curled tightly in the fetal position, they shook and convulsed as they lay sweating in their charcoal and dingy white, striped jumpsuits. They grabbed and hit at their extremities as the pain so obviously coursed through their thin, drug-riddled bodies. My gut wrenched as I tried not to stare at them though their anguish was so great they seemed completely unaware of our presence above.

I immediately thought of Addison and how many times he had endured withdrawal. Probably more times than I am aware of. At least he didn't have to do it in jail. Opiate withdrawal seemed horrible enough in your own pajamas, in your own bed, with your own pillow and your family by your side holding your hand and waiting on you. I agonized over those poor souls that I witnessed going through such misery all alone on pleather mats atop metal cots surrounded by cinderblocks. They were alone, even with the guards around, and it was their solitude that distressed me the most. They had no one there who loved them. I grieved.

We were on our way back down the stairs returning to the Sherriff's office when he stopped, looked up at my mother and me, and said, "Yesterday morning I was on my knees in prayer during my morning quiet time. I asked God to please send me someone to help these people. I asked him to please send me someone who is finally going to make a difference, and then you called me, and now you're here. I just wanted you to know that."

"Thank you," I replied through my tears that I willed not to fall. "I haven't quite figured out what I'm supposed to do yet, but I'll do it once He tells me." I knew then that I had found a valuable ally and a new friend in Jack Stockton.

Before mom and I left, the sheriff pulled from his desk drawer two sheets of white paper stapled together and handed it to me. "You can read this now, but it's really for later." Not sure what I should do, I thanked him, folded the papers, and tucked them into my purse. "You realize this isn't going to be an easy road?" he asked. "There are going to be a lot of people who are not gonna be happy with what you are doing. You'll be stepping on a lot of toes. You'll be hitting people in the wallet. You'll be taking people's drugs away. You've got my support. I'm only a phone call away. You can do this. You're gonna do this *if* you don't give up." After a few short hours with the Sherriff we were past hand shaking and I gave him a big hug goodbye. He bent down and gently squeezed my little mom around her shoulders, bringing her to tears once again. Mom and I requested all of the information from Jack so that we could go visit Toby in the Fentress County Jail, which we began to do on a monthly basis.

I opened the papers that Jack had given me once we were back on the road to Knoxville. It was a story.

The Fern and the Bamboo

Once day I decided to quit. I quit my job, my relationship, my spirituality. I wanted to quit my life.
I went to the woods to have one last talk with God.

"God," I said, "can you give me one good reason not to quit?"

His answer surprised me. "Look around," he said. "Do you see the Fern and the Bamboo?"

"Yes," I replied.

"When I planted the Fern and the Bamboo seeds, I took very good care of them. I gave them light; I gave them water. The Fern quickly grew from the earth. Its brilliant green covered the floor. Nothing came from the Bamboo seed. In the second year the Fern grew more vibrant and plentiful, and again nothing came from the Bamboo seed. But I did not quit on the Bamboo." He said, "In the third year, there was still nothing from the Bamboo seed, but I would not quit. In the fourth year, again, there was nothing from the Bamboo seed, but I would not quit." He said, "Then in the fifth year a tiny sprout emerged from the earth. Compared to the Fern it was seemingly small and insignificant. But just six months later the Bamboo rose to over 100 feet tall. It had spent the five years growing roots. Those roots

made it strong and gave it what it needed to survive. I would not give any of my creations a Challenge it could not handle." He said to me, *"Did you know, my child, that all this time you have been struggling, you have actually been growing roots? I would not quit on the Bamboo. I will never quit on you. Don't compare yourself to others."* He said, *"The Bamboo had a different purpose than the Fern, yet they both make the forest beautiful. Your time will come,"* God said to me. *"You will rise high."*

"How high should I rise?" I asked.

"How high will the Bamboo rise?" He asked in return.

"As high as it can?" I questioned.

"Yes," He said. *"Give me the glory by rising as high as you can."*

I left the forest and brought back this story. I hope these words can help you see that God will never give up on you.

Never regret a day in your life.
Good days give you Happiness.
Bad days give you Experiences.
Both are essential to life.
Keep Going....
Happiness keeps you Sweet.
Trials keep you Strong.
Sorrows keep you Human.
Failures keep you Humble.
Success keeps you Glowing.
But Only God keeps you GOING.

---Crystal Laymance

legislative plaza

Addison had been gone only 36 days when, in response to my considerable number of emails, in conjunction with the help of Karen Pershing from the Metropolitan Drug Commission, I had successfully procured an appointment with Senators Ken Yager, Becky Duncan-Massey, and Randy McNally at the Legislative Plaza in downtown Nashville on February 7, 2012. Prior to our first of many trips to our state capitol, I began collecting as much data as possible and spent the majority of my days researching the prescription pill epidemic that had taken up residence in our state. I knew that I was going to need more than my personal tragedy to garner the attention necessary to facilitate real change. I needed facts, numbers, statistics, and I had plenty of help.

Information began pouring in from the thousands of A.D.D.I.S.O.N. Facebook members. Articles from local, state, and national newspapers were shared and re-shared among us with headlines that read, "Interactive: An Addict's Journey from Kentucky to Florida - Medical writer Laura Unger looks at the trip Kentucky drug addicts make through Knoxville to Florida's Broward County, where cash-only pain clinics have sprung up to meet the demands for prescription drugs." Stories such as "Knoxville Man charged in 6.5

Million Dollar Pill Operation" and "Dying to get High: East Tennessee Choking on Accidental Drug Overdoses," circulated in the *Knoxville News Sentinel*, and "Sales of Oxycodone in Florida Dropped 20 percent in 2011 Thanks to Legislative Efforts," from The Partnership at Drugfree.org began to flood my inbox.

What ultimately became even more valuable to me than the news reports were the thousands of personal impact stories from my army of new friends and supporters. Following each news article was page after page of comments from members of Addison's Facebook group with their horror stories:

C.R.: I know I don't know you, but my friend recommended this page to me. I am from Chattanooga and have many friends who are addicted to OxyContin. They would go downtown and pick up a homeless person and pay for them to get an MRI, and they would send them into the clinic to get all of their medicine. It usually consisted of a ridiculous amount of OxyContin, of which they would sell half. I have seen kids steal thousands and thousands of dollars' worth of stuff to pay for these pills, and the pills are everywhere! Someone needs to stop this because it is hurting our society in Tennessee with all of these super addictive pills being practically handed out.

K.G.: I think what you are doing is wonderful. I just read in today's Athens paper where a man dressed up as his deceased sister just to get her pain meds from the pharmacy. It is so sad the lengths that this addiction will make some people go to.

A.P.T.: My twin sister allowed drugs to consume her life and lost three children by choosing the drugs over them. She even resorted to prostitution to pay for her addiction.

I was amazed. Was there anyone that this plague had not infected? It wasn't long before the stories all began to sound the same, with varying degrees of severity: prescription, addiction, theft, fraud, incarceration, destruction, repeat, death. I was told stories of people popping their own joints out of place in the pain clinic parking lot or having a friend beat the hell out of them the night before, all in the name of acquiring that almighty prescription. I was informed of the most notorious pain clinics across the state in which canine, feline, or even equine x-rays were accepted and introduced into patients' medical records. What's worse were the stories of people breaking their animals' bones on purpose in order to take their pet to the veterinarian so that they could have an x-ray to use in the first place.

The pain clinics were completely out of control and had become purely "for profit businesses." A $400 cash fee, no I.D. or proof of insurance required, no proof of injury or medical need for pain management, walk-in, walk-out, "you got the cash, we got your stash," BUSINESS. Many patients who had become addicted to prescription pills after entering the clinic for legitimate pain management attempted to quit cold turkey only to be bombarded with solicitation phone calls. "We haven't seen you in a while at the clinic. Just calling to make sure you don't need anything. You aren't hurting are you? Are you sure you don't need anything? You know where we are if you need any more medication!" Disgusting.

I had to do something! I had story upon story of the unregulated pain clinics taking advantage, exploiting the vulnerable, and making big bucks doing it—sometimes up to $40,000 per week. Where were the legitimate pain clinics that actually cared about their patients? After dozens of phone calls I learned that hospitals were the most regulated, and by that I mean SELF-regulated. With the buzz that my Facebook page had generated, I easily found a hospital pain clinic employee all too eager to help. I gathered a list of their self-regulations that most in-house, hospital, pain management clinics use in order to assist their patients with legitimate pain while attempting to keep their patients from becoming dangerously addicted to their prescribed medications. It was with that list, a copy of the A.D.D.I.S.O.N. logo, a stack of papers filled with personal addiction stories from Facebook, and my mother, that I headed off to the Legislative Plaza to beg for help.

When Karen Pershing from the Metropolitan Drug Commission offered to accompany us to Nashville, we readily agreed and were relieved at the mention of following her in our own car. We did not want to asphyxiate her with cigarette smoke before we reached our destination. I pulled my hair into a bun and wore an Ann Taylor pantsuit, hoping to make the right impression in my frazzled state. I nervously chatted with my mother as we cruised down Interstate 40. My mother, still suffering from the trembling after effects from the trauma of finding my brother's lifeless body only a month prior, sat anxiously in the passenger seat as I drove. We left Knoxville with ample time to reach downtown Nashville, which was just two hours west. The adrenaline surged, however, as I approached what appeared to be miles of lit brake lights in front of us midway through our trip. When our search for alternate routes via GPS failed, we had no choice but to sit and wait in the endless traffic that threatened to impede the most important meeting of my life thus far.

We swerved into downtown Nashville at 1:00 p.m. local time, and our designated meeting time with the senators was only moments away. The streets of downtown were bustling, and my heart began to race as we continued up, up, up, each floor of the parking garage. "Are there not any freakin parking spots?" I was beyond flustered by the time we finally did manage to find a place to park. The three of us scurried across the street, my heels way too high for that kind of trek. The Legislative Plaza is a very imposing and regal building, beige and grey in color and surrounded on all sides with hundreds of yards of concrete, granite, and possibly marble. One façade was adorned with impressive columns, and the American and Tennessee Flags flew high above the cylindrical-shaped tower on the roof.

"Didn't you say you had been here a bunch of times before?" I asked Karen as we made our third trip around the building that was seemingly locked up like a fortress. We could see people filing down the hallways through the windows and the glass doors as I frantically ran to each one pushing and pulling and shoving to no avail. We were locked out. I met several people's gaze through the glass as I desperately mouthed pleas for help, but like in a dream, they kept walking. I know they saw the frantic look on my face, yet no one offered to help. I had forgotten that in preparation for our meeting and so as not to appear unprofessional, I had preemptively silenced my phone before leaving the car and would not realize until much later that Senator Massey's secretary had been calling me to find out where we were since we were now nearly fifteen minutes late. Fifteen minutes! I don't do late. My mother doesn't do late. When people are late it annoys me, and now I was one of those people. I couldn't believe this was happening, and just when I thought things couldn't get any worse one of my pant legs got caught on the toe of my shoe causing me to trip up a set of concrete stairs and nearly rip my suit and crush my face.

I broke out into hives. I could feel how flushed my face was and just knew that my neck was covered in big red splotches. A passing policeman must have thought we were insane as we began yelling and flailing our arms at him to help us. "How do we get into the building?" we shouted. He directed us all the way back to the street corner and down a flight of stairs. As we walked through a very wide concrete tunnel, imagine our surprise to learn that the main entrance was UNDERNEATH the building. You'd think they'd have a sign or something. After practically throwing my purse at the security guard I made my way through the metal detector and while waiting for my mother and Karen to be cleared, I reached for my phone in my purse to see just how late we were, "Oh, my God," I said. I thought I was going to vomit when I realized that not only were we more than twenty minutes late. On top of that I had missed nearly a dozen calls from the Massey's office. My mouth still open, I looked up and saw a woman walking toward us through the crowd. Her eyes met mine and seeing my frantic panic she knew exactly who I was. "Jessica?" she bellowed over the mass of people darting around us.

"Yes!" I shouted back and jogged up to meet her while concluding that my feet had to be bleeding inside my black leather heels.

Senator Massey's secretary Debbie seemed relieved to have found us yet thoroughly annoyed at our tardiness. Weaving in and out of crowds of people, she guided us down the long hallways to the elevator while I profusely apologized and attempted to reassure her that we were NEVER late. We burst into the office. All three of us were out of breath. I was certain that I still had the hives on my neck, and I just knew that under my suit jacket I had completely perspired through my shirt. What a fabulous first impression. I approached the table where the three senators sat, swallowed my pride, and stuck out my hand to introduce myself and my mother. Again, the apologies flowed from my lips though I didn't want to waste much more time going through the details of the traffic, and the parking, and the "where the hell is the front door?"

We got right to business as I thrust in front of them the A.D.D.I.S.O.N. logo, showed them the list of regulations that I felt needed to be put into place, and began telling them all about my brother, the Facebook page that I had created, and the thousands of Tennesseans who needed help. No one spoke as they studied my proposals. We sat in awkward silence until Senator Yager leaned forward and pulled off his glasses, "Well, Jessica, it seems that you have a lot of good recommendations here, and that you have done your homework. Obviously, you are a little late to get all of this in for this legislative session, but we'd be happy to start looking at this list next year. It's quite a list you have here, so hopefully within three to five years you'll be able to successfully implement all of this."

"Wait. What? Too late? Three to five YEARS? I'm sorry Mr. Senator, but we don't have three to five years. People are dying! People are dying at a much more significant rate than you obviously are aware of. The latest statistic from the Tennessee Medical Association that I read stated that we had lost 1,500 Tennesseans in the last decade from an accidental drug overdose, and that number is just plain inaccurate. We've lost more than that in the last six *months*!"

I had to stop and take a deep breath. Any hope that I had of the hives going away went out the window. I couldn't understand how I had arrived in Nashville just weeks after the year's session had started, yet I was too late. But like I said, it's embarrassing to admit how little I knew about government and the legislative process. Had it not been for Senator Becky Duncan-Massey continually taking me aside, calming me down, and answering my questions, I'm not sure what I would have done. My meeting lasted all of about seven minutes, and I left the room having no idea how I should feel. Becky escorted us from Senator Yager's office and led us back down the elevator and down the hall to her office. She explained that I was too late for this year because we needed time to draft the legislation and then send it on its way through the senate and house committees to be voted on, and I needed time to secure those votes. Apparently, I had lots of lobbying to do, and even more research. The senators had been kind, and you could tell that they felt for us and our situation, but I was going to have to bring a lot more to get through to all of the Nashville suits.

Becky showed us her office; she was excited, having just been elected to her first term as state senator. She handed my mother and me each a copy of a blue hardback book.

"Want a Blue Book?" she said expectantly.

"Sure!" I replied as my mother and I shrugged our shoulders at each other while Becky wasn't looking. *What the hell was a Blue Book?* we thought. We accepted the books to be polite, having no clue how necessary the little volume would become in our future. Becky explained some to me about the process that I was facing. She told me about the opposition that I may be up against and reminded me about how very slowly our legislative system truly works, but she reassured me and encouraged me that what I was proposing was legitimate and necessary. I was thankful from the very beginning that God sent me to Becky. I knew she would be the one I could go to, and the one I could ask all of my ignorant questions. She saw the fire and the passion and the drive within me for what they were, rather than passing them off as simple impatience. She got me, and she helped me more than I think she realizes.

For once I welcomed the brisk air of February as we exited the Legislative Plaza that afternoon. I had been sweating for what seemed like hours. I could not wait to take off my shoes. I had never been so happy that I had the foresight to bring a pair of pajamas to change into for the ride home. My mother and I discussed the events and tried to calm ourselves from the rush of the day as we headed back to Knoxville. It would take us both quite some time to get over being more than twenty minutes late to somewhere so important, but by the time we were near home, we were both laughing hysterically at the thought of us trying to find the damn front door.

I pulled out my laptop the moment I arrived home. I had to post on Addison's Facebook page about our trip. Everyone had been praying and waiting.

Nashville Update:
Thank you to Senators Massey, McNally, and Yager for sitting down with me to discuss this issue.

What I learned:
How to get INTO the Legislative Plaza Building? (Finding the front door is not as easy as one would think!) Seriously, the meeting was positive but as a very impatient person by nature I learned that this is a PROCESS, and it takes time. The senators said they would have me return, they listened to what I had to say, and they agreed with the regulations I proposed.

What I will do:
First of all, NOT give up. Knowing that this problem didn't start overnight, and that it will not end overnight is frustrating but true and something that we all must accept. But, we ARE moving in the right direction, and I feel that the legislative system will allow me to assist in any way that I can.

What YOU can do:
If you live in the state of Tennessee and have concerns about the issue, which I know most of you do, send an email of your own to Senator Yager and mention that we need regulations in place to help alleviate this problem. You can mention my name, this Facebook page, and anything else that you think would help those in office understand how BIG this problem is.

The Regulations I proposed:
1. Patients must have a primary care physician.
2. Must have a Tennessee state ID with photo.
3. Must have a doctor referral AND a current MRI, X-RAY, or CT scan – or any other PROOF of illness or injury.
4. Clinic must check the statewide medical database before treating a patient to check for doctor shopping.
5. First visit and subsequent RANDOM drug testing to check levels.
6. NO MORE 60-90 DAY PRESCRIPTIONS (30 day dosage maximum).
7. Use an Addiction Risk Assessment Form for each patient.
8. A physician must be ON SITE when the clinic is open for operation.

I will keep you all updated as we progress. Please keep sharing this page and keep awareness in the forefront. The more people I have behind me supporting our goals, the better. Thank you all for everything that you have done to help. I appreciate it more than you know.
Much Love,
Jessica

addison facts

I posted on Addison's Facebook page every single morning. When I wasn't giving instructions, requesting research assistance, or posting about a legislative or media appointment, I poured out every single thing that came into my mind about Addison. Those posts became known as "Addison Facts," and the thousands who read my daily posts began to love them. Over time, literally, hundreds of Addison's friends and acquaintances wrote to me publicly and privately via Facebook and email to tell me how special he was or to share memories of their own with me. I did not encounter one person who did not say that Addison was truly one of a kind. It was obvious that everyone else saw in him what I had seen in him, and though he could truly be a giant pain in the ass and overly dramatic at times, he was genuine. His loving heart and caring personality were apparent to all, and his incomparable humor was always noteworthy. He clearly made an impression on every person he encountered. I received messages from people who had met him only one time.

    I wrote everything that I could remember about him so that the thousands of others who never had the opportunity to know him would feel as if they had. Deep down I also believe that I wrote about him so that the memories and facts about him that were so fresh in my mind around the time of his death would not fade. I wanted a record of who he was, at least as much of him as I could remember, so that in a sense he would never be forgotten. People began commenting that each day they looked forward to my Addison Facts and that through them they got to know him. They assured me that my love for him was obvious.

February 10, 2012

Addison Sharp was born on October 24, 1989. He was ten years my junior. I begged for a little brother or sister for years before he was born. I helped my parents feed him, bathe him, change his diapers, and play with him, continuously. He was the cutest baby---a portrait studio asked if they could hang his picture in the lobby as an advertisement after we had photos made.

He never learned to crawl. He bumped around backward on his back to get around before he learned to walk.

We used to call him "Bug."

He had the fattest little cheeks, and I squeezed them all the time until he was about twelve. I would say, "I'm gonna chub those cheeks!" and he would run from me.

He would float on his back in the pool and the ocean with my mother's hands just below the surface when he was less than a year old.

When he was about two, we would look in the sky and say, "What's that?" and he would say, "The MOOOOOOOOOOOON!"

When he was moved out of his nursery and into his "big boy" room he would sneak out of it and into my room on a regular basis.

When he got a little older we had a secret time he called "munchie nights." I would let him stay up late in my room on the weekends, and we would eat chips and cookies and watch movies---usually *The Sandlot*.

I have memories of my brother's entire life because I was there the day he was born, and I was there the day that he died. I just wanted to let everyone know he was a real person. A genuine and sweet person. He made some bad choices, and because of his disease, it cost him and us everything. We miss him every second of every day. I will continue in future days to tell you facts about who he was. For much of my life, he was everything to me.

February 12, 2012

Addison had strange eating habits. He would eat salad, fried clams, and cottage cheese when he was little, but would never eat a hamburger or hotdog.

He would make chocolate milk with Hershey's syrup and put more syrup in the glass than milk. (Even when he was 22).

At the age of five while on a fishing trip with my grandparents, he threw out the line and accidentally hooked my grandfather in the back. He then told my grandmother, "It's okay Mimi, Papaw said I would make mistakes."

Addison and I used to get into a cardboard box and slide down the stairs.

Also at age five, on Christmas morning he woke my parents before sunrise by saying, "Well, we're in trouble now! Santa left us a dog cage and we don't even have a dog!" (My parents were hiding an eight-week-old puppy in the bed with them, though he didn't know it yet).

I took him all over the neighborhood with my friends to go trick-or-treating for years.

For most of his life, even up to right before his death, he would say, "HOW much do you LOVVVVVE me? Will you make some mashed potatoes for your favorite brother that you love more than ANYTHING?" Call it charm or manipulation, he was great at it.

When he was three, he accidentally broke my front tooth with a yardstick when he jumped off the couch pretending to be a Ninja Turtle.

He LOVED the Power Rangers and banana Popsicles.

He had a stuffed animal, Ernie, from *Sesame Street*, which he accidentally dropped into the Tiger Pit at Busch Gardens. It was such a tragedy for him that a zoo keeper retrieved his "E."

After leaving the dinner table to go to the bathroom in a restaurant in Nassau one Christmas, I found him downstairs minutes later in a room full of adults in the limbo line (he was nine).

These are just a few more of the thousands of memories I have about my brother. It seems like I can connect everything that I see to a memory of him. That's why I always say, "He's everywhere I look." I know he isn't here; he is a Saint, in Heaven, with Christ, where the worries of this world are long gone, and he isn't struggling but is blissfully happy.

I know I will see him again one day, but right now it just seems like a really long time before I get to.

February 14, 2012

I helped Addison with his homework from the time he entered school until the last month before he died.

When he was three or four he was jumping on my parents' bed singing, "got a TRICYCLE, broke all to pieces, and it can't be fixed!" (The funny thing was he never had a tricycle, and we never knew where he came up with that one).

He also used to sing, "Got a rocket, in his pocket, be cool boy!" (To our knowledge he never saw *West Side Story* either).

Addison was diagnosed with ADHD when he was fifteen.

The Ph.D. who did his testing said that his IQ was close to 140.

My husband and I taught him how to drive.

Addison was a mama's boy from Day One.

I met my husband when Addison was six. He went on many dates with us.

During an argument before we were married, Sam said to Addison, "Geez, WOMEN. You can't live with them, and you can't live without them." Addison replied, "I know! How are we supposed to eat?"

Addison used to witness the Gospel and the Word of God to neighborhood children beginning at around age ten.

Addison loved to play paintball; he was on the team for UT.

He was the Captain of the Bowling team at Knoxville Catholic High School and had a bowling average around 250.

I am just writing memories as they come. Some are from childhood; some are from the recent past. Little things that I see trigger them. If you ever got a chance to know him, you knew it was a privilege. Please keep sharing his page. I appreciate you all.

February 15, 2012

Addison loved Mayfield Milk as much as I do. Together we could finish a gallon in a day.
Addison and I used to climb into the bottom of my mother's linen closet to jump out and scare her when she got out of the shower. We both thought it was hilarious. She didn't.

He would always order his pizza with cheese only, but with extra cheese.

We would often see celebrities in the Bahamas at Christmas. When he was ten he made friends with Dr. Dre's son. I made him go ask if I could take his picture, and Dr. Dre happily agreed.

The last celebrity we met this past Christmas was Dave Chapelle. Addison could do an almost flawless impression of him.

My husband and I would play pool basketball with Addison and his friends in my parents' pool during many summers.

Addison made friends wherever he went, literally, everywhere.

After my horseback riding accident in 2009, I stayed at my parents' house for almost four weeks with many broken ribs. Addison lay in bed with me almost the entire time. We watched six seasons of *House* on DVD, and he begged me to move back home when I was well enough to leave. Sometimes I had to make him leave the room because he had me laughing so hard, which was not fun with broken ribs.

My mom and I taught Addison to play card games. Canasta and Spite and Malice were his favorites, and he always wanted to play.

Addison was the heaviest sleeper that I've ever known. When he started UT, I bought him the Sonic Boom Alarm Clock. You could hear it from the street, and it had a buzzer that shook his pillow. He STILL slept through it.

February 20, 2012

Even though Addison was an animal lover, he forgave Michael Vick of his crimes against dogs. (This was something I could never do, and he teased me about it). He would say, "Come on Jessica, you've given me a thousand chances when I've messed up, so you can't give this guy a second one? Everyone deserves that."

Our late Great Dane, Heidi, would only approach TWO guys. EVER. She was skittish in general, even at almost 140 pounds, but was afraid of men for some reason, even though we adopted her at eight weeks old. She loved my husband, of course, but she also LOVED Addison. She would always try and sit her big body into his lap.

February 22, 2012

I regret that I didn't know HOW HARD Addison struggled every single day against his addiction.

He assured me and promised me by continuously saying, 'I'm fine, please don't worry about me, I'll be okay, I can't stand you worrying about me."

I made him promise me he would call me if he was hurting and needed help.

He called when he was in trouble or upset.

He didn't call when he was battling with trying not to take pills or when he was "physically" hurting without them. He didn't want me to worry any more than he already knew I was.

Addison was heartbroken every time that he disappointed us. He never wanted to do that.

I wrote Addison a card or a letter almost every day that he was in rehab, which was more than four months in 2009.

The day I met my husband in 1996, he was wearing a Notre Dame sweatshirt. Over time I seized that sweatshirt as my own. For whatever reason Addison always wanted it. I would let him wear it sometimes, but he always had to give it back. His therapist said that he was beaming when I sent it to him in a box while he was in rehab as a gift and nothing he had to return. It's in MY closet again now. I so wish that it weren't.

The pillow he was sleeping on when he died, which I have slept on every night since he passed, doesn't smell like him anymore.

The "Addison smell" in his closet is overwhelming, wonderful, and heart-wrenching all at the same time.

Sometimes I miss him so much that I fear my heart will stop, my eyes will swell shut, my legs will no longer carry me, and my mind will leave me completely. Addison is perfect at this very moment. He doesn't cry, hurt, or struggle anymore, and every day I try to be happy for him despite how horrible I feel.

Please keep sharing his page. Addison would tell you that no matter how long this takes or even if you think it will kill me, "You don't know my sister." I won't give up, but I need your continual help to grow this page. Thank you to everyone who has shared it.

February 24, 2012

I made a grilled cheese sandwich today. It is the one food item that Addison ate more than any other in his entire life.

Every time Addison would spend the night with me, he slept on the couch. He always had to have two pillows and a pale green flannel sheet. The blankets were too hot, and a regular sheet was too cold. (He was very particular about his temperature and comfort level).

Addison made fun of me for years when I accidentally sliced my finger open with a butter knife. Yes, it can be done.

Addison watched *Sports Center* 24/7. He knew so much about every sport, even those he didn't watch regularly.

Addison loved the comedian and actor Dane Cook and could imitate him almost perfectly.

Addison's favorite XBOX games were FIFA and Madden. I was always so protective over Addison because he was so much younger, but as he got older, I began to realize how protective he had become over me.

Pillow fights were a regular occurrence, even as adults (but obviously not as much fun because he was bigger and stronger).

My husband used to play football in the front yard with Addison and all of his friends when they were very young. It was Sam against ALL of them, and they still thought it was so wonderful when they beat him.

I don't ever remember a time when Addison couldn't swim. He was in the water from the time he was just months old and was never afraid. In our pool, we would have diving contests with his friends. My parents and I were the judges, and the boys competed against each other.

Every fourth of July we would watch the Fox Den fireworks show.

While Addison and I were out one day, we ran into his friend's mom. He introduced me and she told Addison that he had a very pretty sister. I was surprised when we walked out and he said, "You know it would make my life easier if you were just decent looking. I get tired of having to talk about how beautiful my sister is when people meet you."

I wear a necklace now that carries his ashes.

The first week of February I got my first and only tattoo. It's on the right side of my lower back. It is something that I will never regret.

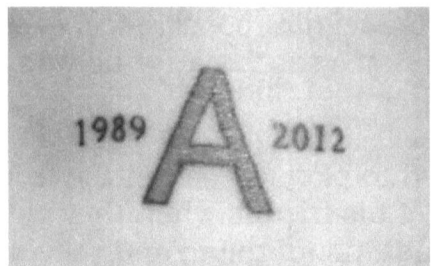

our story

Between the media coverage and Facebook page word of my mission traveled fast. In the months that followed I attempted with great success to join forces with as many groups, associations, affiliations, and higher-ups as possible. I requested meetings with anyone and everyone who would give me an ear for ten minutes. When I was not meeting with members of the legislature, law enforcement officials, or medical staff, I was traveling around Knoxville and surrounding counties for speaking engagements at churches, youth groups, schools, rehabilitation centers, and special events to share our story.

Channel 6 News continued coverage of my journey, and I also began appearing on televised town hall meetings and talk radio stations. I was eventually featured in an article from Knoxville's local *City View Magazine* and was very surprised when publications such as *The Daily* began calling from New York. I was shocked when a reporter from *Dateline NBC* called for an interview, yet I was not surprised and more than a little disappointed that they ultimately declined to produce an episode regarding our story. Addison's name was everywhere, and I received so much media coverage that total strangers began to recognize me. Rarely, did they remember my name, which I didn't mind because they always seemed to remember his, "Hey! Aren't you Addison's sister?" Our momentum continued to grow; therefore, any invitation that I received to come and speak, I accepted. Public speaking is definitely not something I enjoy, but I did it, over and over again and with relative ease because the message I was trying to spread seemed far more important than any stage fright I might have experienced. The student body of Knoxville Catholic High School, where Addison attended and graduated, was comprised of a little more than 600 students and was one of my first stops on my local speaking tour. Addison was not only popular among his peers but was also a favorite among his teachers and administrative staff, all of whom were gracious and more than welcoming toward my mother and me. Channel 6 accompanied me the morning that I stood at the podium in the gym and clicked through my Power Point presentation and delivered my speech to Addison's high school. I was nervous, though many told me that it didn't show. That presentation became second nature to me, as I would deliver it dozens upon dozens of times. The next several pages are the presentation.

Good Morning. My name is Jessica, and I am here today to speak with you about a very important subject, one that I hope you will listen to very carefully because the information I give you today may end up saving your life, or the life of someone you know.

As Mr. Sompayrac said, I am here to tell you a story about my brother Addison. I am also here to give you some vital information that I hope and pray you will take seriously.

This first slide is a picture of my brother, Addison Sharp who attended school here at Knoxville Catholic. He graduated in the class of 2008, and this is one of his senior pictures. The next few slides will show some family photos, along with some pictures of Addison while he was attending school here.

On October 24, 1989 my brother Addison was born. From as far back as I can remember, I begged my parents for a little brother or sister. Then, two days before my tenth birthday, Addison was born. I loved Addison so much from the moment I first saw him. He was always by my side. Addison called me "Sissy" until he was about eleven years old.

He was never what I would have described as "that annoying little brother." We were always together and that's the way that I wanted it to be.

Addison was highly intelligent. He was sensitively kind. He was hilariously funny. Addison was genuine and has been described as larger than life, charismatic, and EVERYONE's friend. Addison's faith in the Lord was strong from a very young age. He knew what he believed, and he wasn't embarrassed to tell anyone about it.

Addison played football here his freshman and sophomore years, but what he truly fell in love with was bowling. He was the captain of the bowling team, and he loved that his favorite teacher, Mrs. Settlemyer, was the coach. They won the regional championship his senior year and then went on to state.

After graduating from Catholic and before starting college, Addison went to get a summer job. It was at his very first job where he was introduced to pills. Almost all the kids his age working there were taking pills, and the assistant manager was dealing pills out of this facility right here in West Knoxville.

Addison took these pills for the first time having NO IDEA what they were. He didn't have a clue what they would do to him. He tried them because he was immature and was experimenting, as many people your age do. Starting this habit was the biggest mistake of his life, and since you freshmen and sophomores are just beginning your high school careers, I pray that you do not make this same COLOSSAL mistake.

Addison moved into Fox Run apartments while he was working, and his drug friends moved right in with him. They didn't ask my parents if it was okay, and they contributed nothing toward paying the bills. They gave Addison pills for free so they would have a place to live, and they used his apartment as a place to sell these drugs. In the beginning, we had no idea that something was so terribly wrong with Addison. As time went on, however, the signs became apparent.

On January 6 of 2009, Addison overdosed on Xanax. My mother had talked to him that night and called me because she said his speech sounded slurred. She wanted me to call him to see if I heard the same thing. I was panicked when he wouldn't answer the phone, so I called his roommate—his "so called FRIEND."

When I asked where Addison was, the roommate said he didn't know and that he was busy playing a video game. I can't repeat to you all of the words that I said to him, but in essence I demanded that he GET UP and LOOK. I was then told that Addison was in the bathroom. He was on the floor, halfway in the tub and half way out. His roommate assured me that it was fine. He said, "He does this all the time . . . he'll be fine." I knew he wasn't fine. Addison was unconscious. After a few terrifying hours in the emergency room we took Addison home to my parents' house. Three days later, on January 9, 2009, we were on a plane with Addison to Arkansas. He was admitted to Capstone Treatment Facility where he stayed for the next four and a half months. Capstone was an all-boys, Christian rehab center.

At Capstone they do Canine therapy, and each patient receives a registered lab puppy that they tend to and take care of during their stay, and then that dog goes home with the patient to be a best friend for life. This picture is of

Addison and his therapy dog. He named her Sadie. We were beyond excited when Addison came home from rehab in mid-April. He did well and stayed clean for a short period of time.

It was after Addison returned home from rehab, that his "so called friends" gave him his first opiate. This is when our troubles went from bad to worse to a complete nightmare. This is when the compulsive lying began, money started disappearing from my parents' bank accounts, and large unauthorized credit card charges started rolling in.

Here are two pictures of Addison. The first one is of Addison right after he graduated from Catholic, before he started taking pills. The second one is a couple of years into his opiate addiction. The difference is beyond obvious. Addison stood at approximately 5'10" and in the first picture he weighed between 175 and 180 pounds. In the second picture Addison weighed barely 140 pounds. This is just one negative effect of what prescription drug abuse does to your body.

This next slide is a comparison of the myths and facts that have to do with opiate addiction and basically addiction to any drug.

Myth 1: Addiction is considered a weakness in CHARACTER or selfishness.

FACT: Addiction is a DISEASE that deals with brain chemistry.

Myth 2: If a drug abuser witnesses enough destruction, such as losing a job, friends, or deaths of others due to drugs that will "WAKE THEM UP."

FACT: Viewing ill effects may cause sadness and shame but is MINOR compared to the withdrawals and compulsiveness created by addiction.

Myth 3: People who become addicted to prescription pills are uneducated, lower class, or must have some history of neglect or abuse to make them turn to drugs.

FACT: ANYONE can become addicted to prescription drugs; people from every age, race, gender, and socio-economic background.

Addiction is a never-ending cycle. The addict has a craving for the drug, which is linked to memory, which moves on to taking the desired drug. Once an addict has taken the drug and has no more to ingest, he begins to have withdrawal symptoms, which lead to taking more of the drug, which leads to more cravings, and so on...

The emotional cycle of addiction begins with the FANTASY (or craving and thinking about the drug). It moves on to the RITUAL of obtaining the drug (this is just as much a part of the addiction as actually TAKING the drugs: where am I going to get them, how will I get the money, where will we meet, and so on). Then it moves on to the ACTING OUT (of physically ingesting the drug). When all of that is over the addict is left with SHAME. Addicts feel terribly guilty for what they have done, the lies they have told, the money they have stolen. The entire act brings out tremendous shame. But shame isn't enough to never do it again because shortly after the shame comes another craving (or fantasy). It is easy to see from this simple picture how maddening this cycle becomes to an addict. There are three different and specific parts of the brain that opiate addiction affects.

First: Opiates change the brain stem—an area that controls automatic body functions and depresses breathing.
Second: Opiates change the limbic system, which controls emotions to increase feelings of pleasure.
Third: Opiates can block pain messages transmitted by the spinal cord from the body.

Everyone is born with the naturally-occurring neurotransmitter chemical called DOPAMINE. Dopamine creates a pleasure sensation that motivates us to perform certain tasks (example: eating). Using addictive drugs FLOODS your brain with Dopamine—as much as 5-10 times the normal level. Over time, by artificially raising the dopamine level, your brain becomes rewired to think that level is "normal."

The user's brain then requires MORE dopamine than it can naturally produce, and it becomes dependent on the drug, which never actually satisfies the need it has created.

When the body is getting a drug from an outside source, the brain stops making some of its own chemicals, such as dopamine and endorphins that it makes naturally. The brain then becomes dependent on the outside source of drugs.

What that is saying is those little blue things on the diagram called the dopamine receptors get smaller and smaller, making an addict need more and more dopamine artificially. The most concerning problem related to this is that much of the brain chemistry change that occurs here is PERMANENT. Some of the components that I have talked about that increase in levels and decrease in size in an addict's brain stay that way FOREVER.

Simultaneously, as the brain adapts to the drug's presence, the individual using the drugs must take MORE and MORE of the drug to try to reach the same feelings that they got when they first started using. Why can't they just stop? We asked Addison and ourselves this question so many times.

Withdrawals: If these drugs are stopped abruptly, the dependent person will go into "withdrawal" because the body is no longer receiving the outside source of the "chemical" it has grown to expect. Here is a list of the opiate withdrawal symptoms, and I can tell you that they are SEVERE:

insomnia
muscle pain
vomiting
bone and joint pain
restlessness
cold flashes
diarrhea
involuntary leg movements

Most prescription drug addicts look normal. Many people who knew Addison while he was in active addition to opiates had no idea he had a drug problem. On the outside, he looked okay, but inside, he felt terrible and consumed and controlled by addiction. He felt like someone huddled in a dark room with shadows of his own demons just waiting to come get him. I have seen Addison in this exact position, on the floor, rocking himself, and pulling his hair in frustration and torment.

There came a time when the fear of Addison's death, which I carried every day of my life for almost four years, went away. The last six months of Addison's life he was CLEAN. He gained nearly 40 pounds. He made excellent grades at UT, declared his major, and was looking forward to his future.

We were becoming happy again, and I was seeing the Addison that I loved more than anything come back to me.

Addison's last week on this earth was spent in Nassau, where we looked forward to visiting every year for Christmas. We spent that week laughing and enjoying each other's company. As a family, we were comfortable thinking that Addison would stay in recovery.

This is our LAST photograph taken together, on New Year's Eve, 2011, just shy of three months ago.

The very night we returned home from the beach, after six solid months of sobriety, my brother, Addison Sharp, at the age of 22, passed away in his sleep from an overdose of an opiate called Opana.

The cravings had never gone away. He struggled every day, fighting against them in silence. In an instant, he gave in to those old familiar feelings, thinking, *I'll just do this ONE more time.*

And then he was gone.

We will miss Addison forever.

Addison is the FOURTH of his personal friends to die from a prescription drug overdose, including one of his best friends who graduated with him from Catholic.

We have an epidemic in our country, and Tennessee is second only to West Virginia in prescription drug addiction and overdose deaths. After the worst tragedy I have ever experienced in my life, I realized right away that something had to be done.

I created this Facebook page, which I think some, if not many of you, have heard of. I appropriately named it after Addison: *Abolish Drug Distribution Igniting Support of New-Beginnings*. I have thousands of members from every state in our nation and more than twenty countries. Almost everyone on this page is suffering from addiction, knows someone suffering from addiction, or has lost someone to addiction. On this page, I tell them about Addison. I tell stories about who he was, and about my memories... good and bad.

I have also traveled with my mother to the Capitol Building in Nashville three times since Addison's death to lobby senators and state representatives to put laws into place so that prescription drugs are not so easily available on the street.

Addison never obtained ONE SINGLE PILL from a doctor. He got all of them from other kids his age, but the reason he was able to get them so easily is because there are no laws in our state to regulate the prescribing of dangerous prescription drugs. I am working to change that, and I have a lot of support. I hope after today that each of you will visit this page, like it, and then share it with all of your Facebook friends. Please urge them to do the same.

There will be time at the end of this presentation for questions, but I want to give you my email address in case you ever want to ask me something or talk privately.

Before I leave you, I want to read you a poem. Some of you may have heard it before. I have found out that it was not originally written about pills specifically, but about meth. When it was sent to me it literally gave me chills because nothing I have ever heard or read has described what I witnessed and experienced with Addison's pill addiction any more accurately than this:

> I destroy homes, tear families apart,
> take your children, and that's just the start.
>
> I'm more costly than diamonds, more costly than gold,
> the sorrow I bring is a sight to behold,
> and if you need me, remember I'm easily found.
> I live all around you, in schools and in town.

I live with the rich, I live with the poor,
I live down the street, and maybe next door.
My power is awesome; try me you'll see,
but if you do, you may never break free.

Just try me once and I might let you go,
but try me twice, and I'll own your soul.

When I possess you, you'll steal and you'll lie.
You do what you have to just to get high.
The crimes you'll commit, for my narcotic charms
will be worth the pleasure you'll feel in your arms.

You'll lie to your mother; you'll steal from your dad,
When you see their tears, you will feel sad.

But you'll forget your morals and how you were raised,
I'll be your conscience, and teach you my ways.
I take kids from parents, and parents from kids,
I turn people from God, and separate from friends.

I'll take everything from you, your looks and your pride,
I'll be with you always, right by your side.

You'll give up everything, your family, your home,
your friends, your money, then you'll be alone.
I'll take and take, till you have nothing more to give.
When I'm finished with you you'll be lucky to live.

If you try me be warned this is no game.
If given the chance, I'll drive you insane.

I'll ravish your body; I'll control your mind.

I'll own you completely; your soul will be mine.

The nightmares I'll give you while lying in bed,
the voices you'll hear from inside your head,
the sweats, the shakes, the visions you'll see;
I want you to know, these are all gifts from me,

But then it's too late, and you'll know in your heart,
that you are mine, and we shall not part.

You'll regret that you tried me, they always do,
but you came to me, not I to you.
You knew this would happen. Many times you were told,
but you challenged my power, and chose to be bold.
You could have said no, and just walked away,
If you could live that day over, now what would you say?

I'll be your master; you will be my slave,
I'll even go with you, when you go to your grave.
Now that you have met me, what will you do?
Will you try me or not? It's all up to you.

I can bring you more misery than words can tell,
So come follow me, to a life of hell.

The poem is attributed to many sources, but most often to Samantha Reynolds. What's revealing is that it has been shared thousands of times across many platforms.

I have been in your shoes, and I have been your age. I have sat through symposiums and speeches on the subject of drugs, underage drinking, and sexually transmitted diseases. When sitting in your place, I thought to myself, *Oh how sad, but that will never be me.* The lighthearted mentality of individuals your age is thinking, *Things like that happen to other people.* But I am here to tell you that Addison WAS one of you. One of his best friends who died from the same thing a year before Addison went to school here, and he WAS one of you. PLEASE don't let this be you. PLEASE don't do this to yourself and your family.

Some days I don't understand why I am still alive, because the pain of losing my baby brother is the worst pain I have ever experienced. I carry an ache in my heart that never ceases. Please don't travel down this road that too many before you have traveled. I pray that you have heard me today and that you will walk away realizing how serious this is. I pray that you won't play games with your life. Addison tried to, and he lost.

I am not ashamed of my brother. I am not embarrassed about his addiction. He was so much more than an addict. He was wonderful. He was my baby brother, and I will miss him every day for the rest of my life.

the proposal

Looking back through my Facebook posts, it amazes me how much we accomplished in such a short amount of time. Still operating on autopilot from the shock, I worked. I worked relentlessly. I worked from sun up to sun down, day in and day out. I did anything to keep myself busy enough in an attempt to not feel the pain. Following dozens of empty-handed introductions, I printed A.D.D.I.S.O.N. business cards, followed by purple rubber A.D.D.I.S.O.N. bracelets, which were sold and worn across the United States, Canada, and the Bahamas.

 I not only traveled throughout Knoxville speaking to as many people as would listen, but I was also given the opportunity to return to Nashville on several occasions to the Legislative Plaza to testify before one committee or another to help pass other pieces of legislation pertaining to prescription pills. There was an attempt to add my proposed regulations as amendments onto "The Tennessee Prescription Safety Act of 2012," a piece of legislation requiring prescribers and pharmacists to report to and check the Tennessee statewide database when prescribing and filling prescription narcotics. The act was an attempt to curb doctor shopping. Our efforts were ultimately unsuccessful, partly due to the sheer number of regulations that I was proposing, as well as the limited amount of time I had to lobby. There is an art to successful lobbying, and Lindsay was the one to teach me the ropes.

It was during my first phone conversation with Lindsay that I realized we had ridden horses in Pony Club together as children. Being connected with someone my own age, and from my past, however distant, set my mind a little more at ease. It was nice to have yet another person to whom I could ask my ill-experienced questions without feeling totally stupid. She brought me in on another piece of legislation that she was lobbying for. It pertained to tamper-resistant opioids (pain pills that cannot be crushed and snorted or melted and injected). I learned the ins and outs of lobbying by following Lindsay around in circles for what must have been MILES inside the Legislative Plaza as we went from appointment to appointment, office to office, senator to senator, and state rep to state rep. We explained the legislation we were lobbying for, what the bill would accomplish, and asked for their support one vote at a time.

After several days I realized I was going to have a problem. I had a lot to say. A lot. For a process that moves so incredibly slowly, the actual day to day business that is done in the Legislative Plaza is done very quickly and usually in five to ten minute segments as you chase the heels of a senator down the hallway talking like the Micro Machine Man in the commercials from the late '80s. The hallways of the Plaza look like a busy street in downtown Manhattan. How in the world was I going to get everyone's attention so that they would remember who I am and what I was all about? No wonder they told me it would take three to five years to get my regulations passed! My letters and speeches were lengthy. I couldn't express the information with the urgency and importance necessary for them to understand what our state was up against in a chaotic and confused five-minute blurb.

God sent me the solution. It came while I looked through that mysterious "Blue Book" that Senator Massey gave me. Throughout the Blue Book were page after page dedicated to each member of the legislative body for Tennessee. Each page consisted of a color photograph of the member, a short bio, party affiliation, counties represented, and my answer. Written in black and white and staring me in the face were their HOME ADDRESSES. I had seen the stacks of mail on their administrative assistants' desks and couldn't imagine what their email inboxes looked like. There was no way, in that environment, that the legislators could dedicate the time and concentration needed to digest all of the information that the A.D.D.I.S.O.N. community and I would send to them.

It was going to take patience, but it would work. I knew it. It was barely spring, but I knew by May the legislators would be clearing out of the Plaza and returning home for summer break. That's when we would attack—when they least expected it and when they had time and quiet in their own homes to read. However stereotypical this may sound, I did think that the majority of the legislative body consisted of men. More specifically, I figured most of these men had wives, and hopefully those wives would be the ones to collect the daily mail. Who better to convince you to read a letter, written by a grieving sister and a mission-inspired group, mailed to your home, than your wife? All we had to do now was wait until they went home.

I began by mapping out each area in which the prescription drug epidemic was negatively affecting our citizens and society at large and decided that we would dedicate a separate letter to each topic in three-week intervals. This would allow us to conduct proper research on each topic and give the legislative members time to read and absorb our findings before receiving the next letter. For each topic the Facebook members who were Tennessee residents and wished to participate were asked to send either written letters, emails, or both to the members' homes.

 I knew that most people did not own a trusty Blue Book like I did. I also knew that most people would not or did not have the time to be looking up the names and addresses for 99 state representatives and 33 senators. So, while we waited for the session to be over for the year, I made an Excel cheat sheet of names, numbers, and addresses (physical and email) for my A.D.D.I.S.O.N. members. I created a template for our first letter, complete with an outline of everything they needed to include when drafting their own. To keep the continuity among our group, I created A.D.D.I.S.O.N. letterhead that our members could print and use for their correspondence. Before we began, the only other thing that my proposed legislation needed was a name, and thus, *The Addison Sharp Prescription Regulatory Act of 2013* was born.

 Once everyone was organized, and we knew that the legislators were settled in at home for their break, we began. On cue, we all drafted our first letters and subsequently mailed and emailed them to each member's home during the same week.

Dear _____,
My name is Jessica Sharp Akhrass. I am writing to you about a very important issue that not only took the life of my precious little brother, ADDISON, but also is taking the lives of literally an entire generation of people. The prescription pill epidemic is nationwide, but in Tennessee we are at the very top of the list, only second to West Virginia in overdose deaths and numbers of individuals addicted to opiates. My

22-year-old brother died January 2 of this year after a four-year battle with prescription drugs.

I called Senator Becky Massey about ten days after his death so that I could ask for her help to alleviate this problem since Addison was the FOURTH of his "personal" friends to die from this in the last three years. Becky suggested that I create a Facebook page for Addison. I named it after my brother with an appropriate acronym: A.D.D.I.S.O.N. (*Abolish Drug Distribution Igniting Support of New-Beginnings*). Since its inception, the Facebook page has grown to have over 5,500 members and reaches approximately 20,000 people in shares and re-shares per week. Over all, the page has been shared with over one million people.

During the last legislative session I worked with Senator Ken Yager regarding the "Tennessee Prescription Safety Act of 2012." I presented to Mr. Yager a list of eight regulations that I had discovered from researching LEGITIMATE pain clinics such as Tennova Health Care. Implementing the statewide database as a "mandatory" practice was ONE of those eight regulations. Senators Yager, McNally, and Massey have assured me that in the upcoming legislative session we will tackle as many of the other seven regulations on my list as we can.

I want to go ahead and present to the rest of you that list. The Addison Sharp Prescription Regulatory Act of 2013 includes the following regulations regarding pain clinics and the prescribing of narcotics.

- A. No more 60-90 day prescriptions written. They must be reduced to a 14-30 day limitation. (Of course, cancer patients and the terminally ill are excluded, and the only drugs that will be restricted are OPIATES).
- B. There must be a physician IN the building 100% of the time that the clinic is open.
- C. Patients must have a current and valid form of identification.
- D. Patients must have EITHER a primary care physician OR doctor referral to the clinic.

E. Patients must have a CURRENT MRI, X-RAY, CT SCAN, or SOMETHING that validates their injury or REASON for being prescribed narcotics on a regular and long-term basis.
F. Each clinic needs to be equipped with and USE the "Addiction Risk Assessment" form. This questionnaire asks about family history of addiction and lifestyle questions to gauge the "likelihood" of someone having the genetic predisposition for addiction.
G. First visit and subsequent RANDOM urine testing to not only check for illegal substances, but to also insure that the drug that is being prescribed is ACTUALLY in their system and not simply being sold on the street for profit.

As the founder of this group and the leader in the cause, I know that there are rebuttals that can be offered for each and every one of the regulations listed. Trust me. I know what they are and have an adequate response to each of them. Since my brother's death I have dedicated my life to the research of this problem that is killing our youth EVERY DAY.

I, along with the other members of A.D.D.I.S.O.N., will be sending you further information as far as cost savings, not to mention the LIVES saved, from passing this bill.

-You will be given the research results from the incarcerations from every sheriff's office in the state.
-You will receive information on the infants born addicted to opiates every day and regarding the extensive extra wing that was required to be built at our very own Children's Hospital in Knoxville to accommodate the massive number of Neonatal Abstinence Syndrome (NAS) babies.
-You will receive information regarding the overload of court cases regarding the children being taken from their addicted parents and placed into foster care.

-There will be information regarding the savings the state will receive from the cost of the THOUSANDS of autopsies performed each year, not to mention state funded rehabilitation centers.
-You will receive information regarding the regulations that FLORIDA put into place over the last year to drastically reduce the death toll in their state.
-You will receive personal stories, many like my own, who have suffered the loss of a bright, young, and talented person like my brother Addison. If you have never endured the loss of someone so young, and so dear, then you are truly blessed.

You should have received in the mail a letter similar to this along with a FOLDER. I am requesting that you place all further correspondence in that folder so that it can be kept organized until next session.

I have already gotten to know many of you who serve our state in the Legislative Plaza in Nashville. For those who do not know me, I want to thank you ever so much for taking the time to read this letter and the many that will follow. Know that as we lose more and more people to this epidemic every day, this will drive me to work harder to do anything I can possibly do to assist you in making the changes that our state so desperately needs.
Sincerely,
Jessica Sharp Akhrass
(Addison's Sister)

Several weeks later this first letter was followed by our second. As with each letter we sent, I gave the Facebook members an outline and a template to follow, but the second letters were our personal stories. This gave everyone the opportunity to share their experiences and gave voices to thousands who, for the longest time, had felt that no one was listening.

Our group effort gave many of them the courage to share for the first time. In *my* second letter I detailed Addison's journey into addiction and the devastating impact that his sudden death had on our family. I encouraged them to take time when reading all of the other letters that were to come because they were more than just stories. They were people's lives. These people were struggling and hurting and desperately needed their help.

more addison facts

February 26, 2012

Addison called me "Sissy" until he was preteen. Though we called him *Bug* when he was a baby, we ended up calling him *A* or *Big A* up until he died (even though he was never that big).

Addison had a strange love for furniture. It's kind of hard to explain; he was always testing out chairs, futons, and beds, and everything had to feel "just right."

Addison could hook up or "rig" any sound system, speakers, components, etc. I don't where he learned any of that, but if anyone in the family was having a hard time with a computer or a TV, they called him.

When Addison spent the night with my husband and me on weekends, he always requested maple bacon and scrambled eggs for breakfast.

Addison stayed with me when my husband went out of town so that I wouldn't be in the house all by myself.

While in the Bahamas one year we ordered the in-room movie *Paranormal Activity*. I don't think that I would have thought that movie was very scary if it weren't for Addison egging me on the whole time. When it was over I said, "I have to pee, but I don't want to get up!" and he said, "I hope when you do I'm not hiding behind that wall when you come back!"

The entire back of his Ford Explorer was FULL of speakers and a giant subwoofer. You could hear him coming a mile away. Any time I hear the thumping of someone's super loud sound system I think of him.

Every time he came to my house he rang the doorbell five or six times in a row KNOWING it would get all the dogs riled up and barking. (He thought that was SO funny and knew I didn't).

Whenever he did something that he thought was hilarious just to aggravate me, I could never stay mad at him. That was impossible.

The stairs that lead up to Addison's room at my parents' house are right next to the garage door. Every time I left their house I would yell, "Bye A! I love you!" and he'd always yell back, "Bye! Love you too!"

Out of habit I've started to yell up to him over the last two months, forgetting for a split second that he isn't there. Sometimes I whisper it to myself just to feel normal.

March 2, 2012

Today is March 2. Today makes two months. In about 30 minutes, two months ago, my mom found Addison in his room, ice cold. I will probably hate the 2nd of every month for the rest of my life.

The other day I found a paper on my computer that Addison emailed me to edit for his Western Civilization class at UT. It was about Christopher Columbus and was dated November 11, 2011. It was hard to read the words on the screen that he had typed. His words. It was the last paper he ever wrote.

Seems like every time I leave the house I see a black Ford Explorer, which is what Addison drove. He loved his truck.

I also see an ambulance every time that I'm out. I didn't have the horror of following the ambulance to the hospital like my parents did, but I can imagine how terrible that was.

In the past few weeks we have received his final death certificate, his autopsy report, and a letter from the organ donation association. It is hard to read your brother's death certificate, especially since I have seen his birth certificate, with his tiny footprints on it, so many times. It's even harder to read his autopsy report. I wanted to have it, but it's so difficult to read how much every organ in your baby brother's body weighed. It said that he had an enlarged heart – anyone that knew him could have told them that. I guess his heart physically was as big as it was figuratively. The only viable organs to donate were his eyes.

Those beautiful, big, brown eyes. We received a letter telling us that the transplant went well and that someone is seeing through his eyes now. The letter read that he had led someone from darkness into light, which was also true about his spiritual walk while he was alive.

Addison had the best laugh. Maybe it seems better now that he is gone. What I wouldn't give to hear it again.

March 5, 2012

Addison graduated from Knoxville Catholic High School in 2008. He wanted to study psychology at UT after he figured out that business was really boring. (I have my minor in business. I told him he would HATE it!)

I'm not exactly sure what I'll do when it's time to renew my phone. I have texts from him that I would never want to lose, especially the ones that say, "I love you."

Addison was an excellent paintball player and was on the UT Paintball Team. He was always trying to teach me "the finger roll," which I was never any good at.

He loved Reese Cups and Oreo cookies.

Everything that required, or even had the possibility of needing, salad dressing was DRENCHED in ranch.
At Christmas at the Atlantis, he and my dad and husband would have ping pong tournaments outside by the pool.

There used to be a movie theatre across the street from our neighborhood, and I often went as his "guardian" to get him into movies he wasn't old enough to see.

I realized the other day that his toothbrush is still in my guest bathroom.

In the very near future it will be the first time ever that my husband goes out of town and I don't have Addison to come stay with me.

A few weeks after he returned from rehab, I had him come with me and pick out two trees to plant in my backyard. The ground back there is so hard and rocky that I was holding the hose to wet the soil while he shoveled as hard as he could. He would later go home and tell my mom, "Well, we got them in the ground, but I didn't have the heart to tell her they aren't gonna make it." Today those trees (one planted for me, one for him) are HUGE. Mine is bigger than his but they have grown big and strong. The two weeping willows will be the hardest thing to leave if we move from this house.

March 9, 2012

Addison could never answer a simple YES or NO question – everything had a very long and elaborate story attached that always started with, "Well…."

Addison showed up at my house two years ago on Thanksgiving having been in a fight. One side of his face and especially his ear were red and swollen; he had an elaborate story about that, too.

Being the older sister, I tried to protect Addison always, but it was nice when he got older and I felt safer having him with me.

Though he didn't need braces, Addison was always self-conscious of his smile. He never showed his teeth when he smiled until my husband did cosmetic veneers for him, and then he smiled from ear to ear showing them off every chance he got. One of his veneers fell off while he was eating something crunchy. I still had that little piece of porcelain in a baggie waiting for Sam to glue it back on when Addison died.

Addison gave good hugs. He would let you hug him for as long as you wanted and he never pulled away too soon.

Addison had friends in practically every county. When he was about eleven, one day we were talking about the "crowd" he was hanging out with. He looked at us in all seriousness and said, "Pfft, please, I AM the crowd!"

We took a family trip once to visit my husband at dental school in Memphis. We spent one night in Tunica, Mississippi, and passed a billboard on the way to the Gold Strike Resort that said, "Johnny Rivers LIVE in concert!" We all wanted to go, including Addison, who had grown up listening to older music like that with me and my parents. We were about fifteen minutes into the concert when ten-year-old Addison stood up and said, "Move out of my way! I can't STAND it anymore!" He pushed through the seated crowd out to the dance floor. He knew the music so well and seeing the other people dancing was driving him crazy. So, the four of us spent that evening dancing to Johnny Rivers LIVE in concert. I will never forget that night.

March 15, 2012

Addison never paid attention to details. EVER. Like when he came home from football practice his freshman year in high school and my mom swore he had someone else's helmet. (But of course, to Addison it was near his stuff in the locker room, and they all look the same anyway...) So, to prove it was his he jammed it on his head and said, "See!" But it took BOTH of my parents to pry his teammates helmet, which was about three sizes too small, back off of his head, almost taking his ears with it. His response was, "Well, I guess that's not mine. Wonder who has mine?"

Our family recently got a Wii. My parents even learned to play, but there was really no point in playing against Addison in ANYTHING, especially bowling because he won every time.

A few years ago, we watched an episode of *House and* there was an actress on the show who was a midget. A little while later the same actress appeared on *Law and Order*, which is one of my dad's favorite shows. Addison looked up and said, "Hey, she plays a midget on this show, too!" He was totally serious, and it took him a second to realize what he had said. We never let him live that one down.

Addison thought it was hilarious to burp in my face. I guess that's just a little brother thing, and I suppose it could have been worse.

Addison shared everything with everyone. His food, his games, DVD's, his clothes, with little to no regard if he got them back.

I recently got a message from a neighbor of his who said one very cold night, he had accidentally locked himself out of his apartment and was attempting to sleep in his car until morning when the apartment office opened so that he could get a new key. Addison saw him, knocked on his car window, and not only invited, but insisted that he come inside and stay the night. "I had never met Addison before that night. We had never even crossed paths in the apartment complex, but there was no way that he was going to let me sleep in my car on a cold night. He invited me in, fed me dinner, we played XBOX, and I slept on his futon in the living room. I am so saddened to hear of his passing. He was literally one of the nicest, most generous people I have ever met."

Addison was a lighter kleptomaniac, and he didn't even mean to be, but if anyone had a lighter lying around, it would eventually end up in his pocket.

I thought it was hilarious to run up to Addison's room when he was sleeping in on the weekends and take a flying leap and land right on top of him. He never thought that was very funny.

Every time I saw Addison I would hug him and kiss him on the cheek or on the forehead and say, "I love you." I did the same every time we said "goodbye."

March 19, 2012

Addison and I were polar opposites in so many ways.

I remember how his second toe was longer than his big toe, and how he bit his fingernails down to the quick.

Unlike my very fine, extremely curly hair, Addison had extremely thick, coarse, straight hair that grew from the crown of his head toward the front. Unlike my face of many freckles, Addison had very few if any. Addison had the prettiest dark skin that tanned beautifully while my porcelain skin just burns, and then gets more freckles.

I remember Addison's voice as a man, his mannerisms and the way he walked. I've already forgotten his little boy voice and his baby laugh. I can hear his voice saying my name perfectly in my head the way it sounded in the last years of his life.

I remember his smell, though as I remove more of his things from his room, they cease to carry that smell with them.

I'm afraid I'm already forgetting so many memories of him that I can never get back.

March 28, 2012

Addison was the quickest witted person I have ever met. You could come at him with anything, and he would have an immediate, hilarious answer. I miss that laugh, and I miss him making me laugh. No one could ever make me laugh the way he did.

During our last trip to the Atlantis, the week before he died, I was standing outside with Addison and my mom smoking a cigarette. There was a young couple in the hallway who couldn't have been much more than eighteen or nineteen years old. They were totally making out on the other side of the glass door that was right next to us. We were trying not to stare, but I said, "Are they going to take that to a room or what?" Addison, being Addison, immediately says, "Yeah, do you want to go to your room with YOUR parents, or my room with MY parents?"

When we were checking out to go home, Addison was steering the fully loaded luggage cart to the front lobby. A hotel employee passed us on the way and said, "Are you checking out?" And Addison, without cracking a smile looks him dead in the face and says, "No man, just taking my luggage for a walk."

April 4, 2012

Before Addison was born I would put my face up to my mother's belly and talk to him. I would lie in bed in between my parents when she was really pregnant and watch him move. Sometimes you could see a little foot, sometimes an elbow, and I was fascinated with watching him change positions in there.

When Addison was born he looked like he had a suntan. He had very dark, almost black hair, which by the time he was two, looked pretty blonde, but then the older he got, the darker it became again.

Addison had the longest eyelashes of any human being I have ever met.

Addison didn't talk very well when he started saying his first words. He had to have surgery when he was two years old to have tubes put in his ears and his adenoids removed. The doctor told my parents that he didn't speak well because he wasn't hearing very well, but the tubes fixed the problem. He began speaking correctly and never stopped talking after that.

I read a Bert and Ernie book about opposites to him no fewer than 5,000 times.

We had a big conversion van in the early 1990s that had a TV and a VCR. On long trips Addison wanted to watch the same *Sesame Street* video over and over, and I can still remember the words to "John Jacob Jingleheimer Schmidt."

He totally freaked out once as a teenager when I tried to pluck his eyebrows. They just looked too big for his face for some reason, and I told him I could fix it. We only did that once. He kept screaming, "Women are crazy! Why would you ever do that more than once? I'm good looking enough on my own. I don't need your help!"

Addison had a scar that was a perfect circle on the right side of his neck from accidentally getting shot at close range with a paintball gun by one of his friends.

Addison always swam under water with his eyes open. After a day of swimming, his huge eyes couldn't have been anymore bloodshot. The only other time that I saw his eyes look that red was when he overdosed in 2009, and when I saw him after he had died.

April 17, 2012

Addison had his very own unique sense of "style." On the one hand he loved anything that was Ralph Lauren, but the little Polo horse had to be the SMALL one. He was very specific about that, and it had to be a shirt that he could match with one of his MANY hats, which he wore backward on his head almost all of the time.

He loved to dress in Khaki shorts, a Polo shirt, and his Birkenstocks, which he also loved, but then sometimes he would pick out the UGLIEST, most brightly colored pieces of clothing that didn't match ANYTHING. He loved neon colors and weird patterns that used to drive my mom crazy.

He wore his Birkenstocks or flip flops all year long, even in the dead of winter.

On our last trip to Nassau, we took a bunch of supplies for Christmas to an AIDS camp that is on the island. While packing the supplies I realized that Addison didn't know how to fold socks. He struggled and struggled with it, and I said, "I can't believe that you are 22 years old and you don't know how to fold socks!" His response was, "Well, I don't see why I need to. I know how to match socks, so I just throw them in there individually and pull out two that match, and most of the time mom does it for me *anyway*, and I don't even WEAR socks most of the time, so that's a skill that I don't think I benefit from learning."

Addison and I were prone to jumping on the beds when we got to the hotel room at the beach, even as adults.

Addison didn't mind my burying him up to his neck in sand.

We fought like any siblings do, but for the most part we always had such a good time together.

I will never forget how much we loved each other. I still won't say aloud I "loved" him because it is past tense. I love him now as much as I did his entire life, and will for the rest of mine.

jail & the morgue

As the summer of 2012 continued, so did our research and letter writing. Though Addison himself had never been arrested, from what I read in the thousands of messages that I received, incarceration was a recurrent theme throughout the lives of the addicted. Yet from every inquiry that I made to every resource I had available to me, or from every news article that crossed my path or television segment forwarded to me, it seemed that no one had any real statistics on how the epidemic of prescription drug abuse was affecting our state in regard to how many people were arrested again and again and again. There were simply no statistics until team A.D.D.I.S.O.N. came along.

I made a list of the 95 counties in the state of Tennessee and posted it on Addison's Facebook page. I instructed the followers to contact the sheriff's office from each county and gather information regarding the currently incarcerated in relation to prescription drug abuse. A few days and hundreds of phone calls later, *voila*: statistics. I then began drafting my letter, which not only introduced the topic of our next wave of correspondence but also included the results of our findings. The followers of Addison's Facebook page followed my letter with their own, but rather than numbers and percentages, they included their personal stories of how prescription pill abuse had led to arrests and incarcerations of their own or of someone they loved.

Dear _____,
Greetings once again to all who serve the state of Tennessee from A.D.D.I.S.O.N.

I came to Nashville to speak with legislators for the first time just weeks after my brother's death in January of this year. I came brokenhearted. I came overwrought with emotion. I shared my brother's story with as many people as would listen, ensuring them that I was just one sister out of literally thousands of others with stories similar to my own. Though I was treated with kindness and sincerity, I realized after a few months of work that we weren't all necessarily speaking the same language. I was speaking the language of love and loss. Those who have not had their lives touched by this epidemic were not understanding me. I, therefore, had to force myself to learn a new language. The language of numbers and budget. This was new to me, having never worked in a legislative capacity of any kind before in my past, but I learned quickly.

The number of LIVES that we are losing every day in our state continues to rise and is something that can never be replaced, nor can a dollar value be placed upon it. I would not wish for any of you to experience the pain of losing someone as young and bright and dearly loved as my brother Addison, and, therefore, cannot expect you to feel the emotions that I do regarding his death from prescription drugs. I have tried to give you a "picture" of what it was like with words, in my second letter, but words hardly do that kind of pain justice.

While you have read about Addison and the heartbreak that his death has caused to many, I will now be sending you raw numbers and budget statistics rather than an emotional story of loss.

This first letter is about drug incarceration statistics. The epidemic we are currently living in is COSTING human lives. That is the most important and painful loss, but I am going to send you statistics revealing exactly what **else** this epidemic is COSTING us, literally.

A.D.D.I.S.O.N. members have been working diligently gathering this information for you. I instructed our group on what information we needed and how to obtain it, and everyone went to work. We have personally called, emailed, and/or faxed ALL 95 sheriffs' offices from ALL 95 counties in our state asking two questions. How many inmates does your jail currently have, and how many of them are incarcerated due to a prescription drug-related charge? Once we explained to each sheriffs' office that we were gathering this information to help implement The Addison Sharp Prescription Regulatory Act regulating illegitimate pain clinics, they literally jumped at the opportunity to help. Some offices even took a few days to do a "physical head count" to make sure their numbers were accurate. As a group, we all worked on this large task together, gathering and reporting data that I have presented for you in this letter.

As you will see, our county jails in Tennessee are FLOODED with inmates arrested and incarcerated because of prescription drug-related charges. Seventy percent (yes **70%**!) of ALL inmates across the state housed in a county jail are there because of or related to prescription pills.

For a quick summary of this extensive chart, I will provide you with some bulleted points below:

•Tennessee currently has approximately 18,000 inmates whose incarcerations are related to prescription drug charges in our "county" jails alone.

•This equates to 70% of our entire state inmate population becoming incarcerated due to or related to prescription drugs.

- According to the sheriffs' offices this number has climbed (and continues to climb) an average of 5-10% per year, over the last 5 years, state-wide.

- 59 of our 95 county jails have an average prescription drug inmate percentage of 60% or above.

- It costs each jail an average of $62.50 PER inmate, PER DAY, to house them. This figure is given assuming that each and every inmate has NO health problems, which we KNOW is not the case.

- Based on this average day rate, our state is spending approximately **$1,125,000.00 PER DAY** to house inmates on prescription drug-related charges.

- Therefore, we have spent approximately **$410,800,500.00** over the last 12 months, and a whopping **$2,000,100,000.00** over the last 5 years.

I ask that you each take a few minutes to review the chart that follows which reveals the results of our research.

COUNTY	TOTAL INMATES	RX DRUG RELATED	%
Anderson	359	233	65%
Bedford	143	52	36%
Benton	74	12	16%
Bledsoe	98	75	77%
Blount	531	377	71%
Bradley	397	260	65%
Campbell	183	156	85%
Cannon	59	30	51%
Carroll	96	54	55%
Carter	260	240	92%

Chester	60	53	88%
Claiborne	211	194	92%
Clay	30	19	63%
Cocke	156	109	69%
Coffee	200	104	52%
Crockett	64	27	42%
Cumberland	200	120	60%
Davidson	3,348	2,880	86%
Decatur	24	11	46%
DeKalb	84	60	72%
Dickson	218	156	72%
Dyer	194	155	80%
Fayette	175	134	77%
Fentress	131	85	65%
Franklin	124	68	55%
Gibson	325	269	83%
Giles	132	108	82%
Grainger	98	68	69%
Greene	380	345	91%
Grundy	40	18	45%
Hamblen	134	114	85%
Hamilton	505	303	60%
Hancock	120	75	63%
Hardeman	156	142	91%
Hardin	140	89	64%
Hawkins	236	220	93%
Haywood	121	24	20%
Henry	188	103	55%
Hickman	107	105	98%
Houston	304	255	84%
Humphreys	41	18	44%
Jackson	140	120	86%
Jefferson	185	178	96%
Johnson	153	98	64%

Knox	960	580	60%
Lake	49	36	73%
Lauderdale	140	121	86%
Lawrence	130	87	67%
Lewis	51	38	75%
Lincoln	116	80	69%
Loudon	148	65	44%
Macon	252	235	93%
Madison	286	149	52%
Marion	109	60	55%
Marshall	154	116	75%
Maury	345	259	75%
McMinn	286	214	75%
McNairy	73	33	45%
Meigs	62	53	85%
Monroe	179	150	84%
Montgomery	600	510	85%
Moore	22	6	27%
Morgan	40	22	55%
Obion	162	39	24%
Perry	49	25	50%
Pickett	157	122	78%
Polk	166	120	72%
Rhea	116	32	28%
Roane	200	190	95%
Robertson	363	Houses federal inmates with county inmates- cannot get accurate results	
Rutherford	932	601	64%
Scott	150	85	56%
Sequatchie	103	55	53%
Sevier	265	199	75%
Shelby	3,662	1,996	55%
Smith	46	22	48%

Stewart	18	17	94%
Sullivan	615	165	27%
Sumner	700	595	85%
Tipton	140	35	25%
Trousdale	53	22	42%
Unicoi	65	33	50%
Union	90	37	41%
Van Buren	31	9	29%
Warren	300	240	80%
Washington	555	362	65%
Wayne	97	85	88%
Weakley	82	20	24%
White	226	124	55%
Williamson	351	42	12%
Wilson	357	292	82%
Total	**24,977**	**16,694**	**67%**

My brother Addison was never arrested. He never spent time in jail. We never had to visit him behind a piece of glass or look at him in that situation and then be forced to LEAVE him there. That, to me, would have been an experience almost as painful as losing him altogether, but now I don't get to see him behind a piece of glass, I don't get to see him at all. For many, that is the only way they get to see their loved ones, and in most cases, it is because of a crime they committed that they would normally have never DREAMED of committing if their bodies had not become biologically dependent.

I hope all of our lengthy yet thorough research in just this ONE area reinforces the need for The Addison Sharp Prescription Regulatory Act for our upcoming legislative session. It has been stated again and again in national news that Tennessee has THE most LAX prescription drug regulations compared to every other state in the nation, hence, the rapidly rising death toll and EXTREME cost to our state budget. I can assure you this epidemic will NOT solve itself. Until we regulate pain

clinics in Tennessee that are fueling the addiction, desperation, and resulting CRIME and DEATH we continue to experience, these numbers will only increase. I ask for your support in the upcoming legislative session to see that we as a state attack this problem head on.
Sincerely,
Jessica Sharp Akhrass
(Addison's Sister)

Though my intention was to give raw numbers and hard data for every instance in which prescription pill addiction was negatively impacting the communities and families throughout our state, I began to realize that sometimes the numbers just weren't there to be found. That definitely was the case when it came to writing the state legislators regarding overdose death autopsies.

    An autopsy. My brother had an AUTOPSY. I had never given so much thought about what all went on during an autopsy until my brother had one, and I had never envisioned myself walking into the morgue to retrieve the report. We could have waited for it to arrive in the mail, but who knows how long that could have taken. We wanted to know what drug had killed him. We wanted to know how much of it he had taken. When my mother found him that morning, with his history, we, of course, assumed it was an overdose, regardless of the fact that he had been clean for so many months. I wanted to see the paper that would show me in black and white what substance ended my brother's life and forever changed the course of mine.

    I was surprised that every horror movie-inspired, preconceived notion that one might have about the appearance of a morgue was actually true. My mother and I took the elevator at The University of Tennessee Medical Center all the way down to the basement. When the doors opened to reveal the darkened hallway, we questioned whether or not we were entering an unauthorized area. There were no receptionists sitting at an information desk nor any direction signs on any of the walls. The faint smell of formaldehyde is actually what led us in the right direction down the long corridor with exposed plumbing overhead.

We wasted no time, once we had the report in hand, getting the hell out of there. The thought of my little brother in that horrible place—dissected, refrigerated—it was almost more than my mother and I could handle. Once we got to the car we ripped open the envelope to find that the drug that had caused Addison's death was something called Opana. What in the world was Opana? In the four years that Addison struggled with prescription pill addiction, I had never once heard of this drug. We would soon learn that this heavy-hitting semisynthetic derivative of morphine is tens of times stronger than the Roxicet that Addison had grown accustomed to, and it took only a pill and a half to kill him.

The legislators didn't want to hear about going to pick up my brother's autopsy report from the morgue, nor did they want to hear about how the smell of the hospital basement lingers in your nose and your clothing. Laws were not going to be written because I had nightmares of that dreadful experience and had to consciously block myself from thinking about everything that had been done to my little brother's body once it arrived in the morgue. They needed facts and statistics, and I learned that "cause of death" isn't something that can exactly be quantified with numbers. Being forced to improvise a little, my internet friends and I called the key medical examiner's offices in our state, among others, to gather as much information as possible so that I could calculate reasonable estimations.

Dear _____,

I am writing this difficult letter today from A.D.D.I.S.O.N. regarding the number of accidental overdose deaths and the subsequent autopsies that follow. It is difficult because I have a copy of my brother Addison's autopsy, which details the dissection and inspection of every organ in his body. It is an understatement to say that reading your little brother's autopsy report is painful; however, I wish to inform you of the inaccuracy of what "studies" are reporting regarding the numbers of accidental deaths from prescription drug overdoses and the number of autopsies performed in our state.

The information, statistics, and quotes used in this letter have been provided by Elizabeth Sherrod (Coordinator of the Tennessee Drug Diversion Task Force), Dr. Eddie Davis, (the coroner for Hamblen County), Dr. Tom Thompson, (the Hamblen County medical examiner), Dr. William Bennett (Roane and Morgan Counties' medical examiner), and Dr. Darinka Mileusnic-Polchan (Director of Autopsy Services at the University of Tennessee Medical Center and the Knox County medical examiner). Dr. Mileusnic-Polchan is also the doctor who performed my brother's autopsy.

If you read the newspaper or online studies reporting on the prescription drug epidemic in Tennessee, you will be grossly misinformed regarding the number of lives that we are losing on a regular basis. Repeatedly, I have seen one statistic in particular that states that we have lost some 1,500 people in the last decade to prescription pill overdoses in Tennessee. I apologize for being blunt, but that number is not only ridiculously off base, but downright absurd. The main reason that this number is so inaccurate is because "we don't have a consistent system of reporting; we don't have a clear picture, but we're not too far behind Florida, and they are losing seven people a DAY" (Sherrod).

Dr. Davis of Hamblen County stated, "I don't know how they (The Tennessee Department of Health) are keeping their numbers, but it's ridiculous! They're at least four times off with their statistics which paint a shallow portrait of the state's most deadly drug problem."

Upon writing an autopsy report, determining the cause of death is strictly up to each individual medical examiner. My brother's autopsy clearly states that Addison's cause of death was "Oxymorphone Intoxication," clearly, a drug overdose. Not all autopsy reports will give you this clear-cut answer. Many accidental drug overdose deaths are listed as natural, accidental, or undetermined, though toxicology will clearly list the single or, in many instances, the "cocktail" of opiates and/or sedatives that caused a person's death. Falling into another "sudden death" category are those deaths listed as respiratory depression, heart failure, or aspiration, but yet again, it is a **drug overdose** which has caused an otherwise healthy twenty-something-year old's heart to fail or caused them to simply stop breathing while asleep. Finally, a long-term prescription pill addict's death may be listed as liver failure, pneumonia, or cardiac arrest, but yet again it is prescription drug abuse that has CAUSED the liver failure or other complications leading to death.

Though there is no consistent nor accurate reporting database to track the number of overdose deaths state-wide, if you speak with medical examiners personally, they are quite clear and concise regarding numbers of cases they have performed themselves. By combining the numbers from individual medical examiners from individual counties across the state, a much more accurate and disturbing number of overdose deaths is revealed.

Following are several examples which will show a much more accurate picture of how many lives have been taken due to prescription drug abuse. In Hamblen county, which has a population of a little over 50,000 individuals, Dr. Davis performed 53 autopsies in which the cause of death was due to a prescription drug overdose in 2011. In the Knoxville Metropolitan Area, which has a population of more than 600,000, Dr. Mileusnic-Polchan performed close to 600 autopsies in which the cause of death was due to a prescription drug overdose in

2011. In Roane and Morgan Counties, which have a combined population of approximately 76,000, Dr. William Bennett performed 68 autopsies in 2011 due to prescription drug overdoses.

Hopefully, from these examples you can see the pattern emerging here that there is a clear correlation between the number of overdose deaths and the population of each county. In 2011, from just FOUR counties out of the 95 that we have in Tennessee, there were over 700 autopsies performed in which the death was caused from an overdose of prescription pills. This number is the combined work of only THREE medical examiners. Therefore, take the statistic that we have lost 1,500 lives over the last decade and DOUBLE it to get only a rough estimate of how many lives we lost LAST YEAR ALONE.

"An M.E. working 8-10 years ago never saw the kind of deaths we are seeing today. We frankly don't get a lot of guidance from the state on the way we are supposed to list these deaths; therefore, the available statistics are exponentially underreported" (Thompson).

The average cost to perform an autopsy in Tennessee is $2,000. According to the statements and records of individual medical examiners, the numbers translate to approximately 3,000 deaths per year state-wide from prescription drug overdoses. Of course, the bill for an autopsy is paid for by the state, which in 2011 was approximately more than $6 million. Six million dollars to perform autopsies for deaths that were LARGELY preventable.

I must reiterate that speaking of the prescription drug epidemic in terms of what it is monetarily "costing" us still unnerves me a bit. It is costing us millions upon millions of dollars. It is costing us money that could very well be spent elsewhere, but it is costing us LIVES. My brother's life was one of those, and you can't put a price tag on that.

Also, keep in mind that not everyone who passes away has an autopsy performed. Of Addison's group of four friends who have died from a prescription drug overdose, he is the only one who underwent an autopsy. A Scripps Howard News Service study concluded that Tennessee performed autopsies in just six percent of all deaths state wide. According to Captain David Honeycutt, chief investigator for the Claiborne County sheriff's office, "If we had to do autopsies on everybody who died of an overdose, it would break this county's budget." When you put into consideration the "actual" number of autopsies performed last year and combine that with the knowledge that autopsies are only performed on 6% of the deaths in our state, it is not difficult to see that this epidemic is drastically larger than most people assume.

Morristown Police Chief Roger Overholt stated, "For the past several years, we've had more citizens in our community to die from overdoses of prescription drugs than from violent acts, car wrecks, and all other illegal street drugs combined." Furthermore, "Our drug overdose rate in Tennessee is 26% above the national average" (Sherrod). That is quite a frightening thought when you consider that prescription drug overdoses are now the leading cause of death nation-wide.

"If this were an infectious disease taking the lives of this many people, everyone would be up in arms" (Bennett). This statement from Dr. Bennett could not be more true. In fact, upon seeing the death toll rise in Florida to the numbers that we are currently experiencing in Tennessee, the Florida State Attorney General, Pam Bondi, declared state of emergency, and I feel we need to do the same. If you mention prescription drugs to just about ANYONE, even someone standing in front of you in the grocery store; they WILL have a story. The question is, are they too embarrassed and ashamed to share it? EVERYONE knows SOMEONE in our state who is affected by addiction.

I hope that this letter, along with previous correspondence that you have received from me and from other members of A.D.D.I.S.O.N. will further encourage your support of The Addison Sharp Prescription Regulatory Act. The number of people that we are losing on a daily basis continues to rise, and unfortunately, will not fix itself. "We have more overdoses per capita than anybody I know of," Roane County

Sheriff Jack Stockton stated. "They are from all ages and all walks of life. There is no family, no economic background that the pill epidemic doesn't reach." Sheriff Stockton, Dr. William Bennett, I, and MANY others blame the overprescribing doctors running "pill mills" and the easy accessibility of painkillers for the spread of addiction across our state. Our proposed bill will help prevent the continuous growth of accidental deaths caused by the prescription drug epidemic, and I kindly ask for your support in the upcoming legislative session.
Sincerely,
Jessica Sharp Akhrass
(Addison's Sister)

chief

Of the hundreds of people I met during my journey, no one seemed to work harder on a regular basis to battle the epidemic of prescription drug abuse than Knoxville's own Police Chief David Rausch. He was kind and overtly welcoming toward my mother and me when we visited his office. He never rushed us, but rather, sat and listened intently as we told our story. Though not an old guy, there was something about his eyes that seemed weary. No doubt it was the wear and tear of a seemingly thankless and exhausting job. He seemed to be genuinely saddened hearing about Addison, and I could tell by his words and demeanor during our conversation that he was a man of faith. I had no idea during this first meeting how much I would come to rely upon Chief Rausch throughout the upcoming legislative session. But looking back it is so evidently clear how God placed the people I needed *at the exact times I needed them* in my direct path.

Like all of his men and women in blue, I started calling him "Chief" right from the beginning, and he never seemed to mind. He explained to my mother and me the devastation that had befallen Knox County and our entire state thanks to prescription pills from his perspective, which I'll admit, was bleak. Chief explained his leading participation in each legislative session. After hearing the extensive list of all that he offered our state between legislation and being the Chief, we had to ask ourselves, when did the man sleep?

I presented him with the list of regulations I was proposing and explained to him our letter-writing approach to the legislative body. He then explained to me one of the bills regarding prescription drug abuse that he was introducing. To my delight I found that there seemed to be a cohesive theme among what we had both brought to the table, and I left our meeting with a slightly renewed confidence in my endeavor. I now had the backing of the Knoxville Police Department and a man who not only had compassion for the afflicted, but also had the experience, competence, and know-how regarding the specifics of drafting legislation. Before my mother and I went home that morning, the Chief prepared to send us on our way with a precautionary warning.

During our time with him, my mother and I had divulged to the Chief that on a pretty regular basis, she and I could be found in one of the county's plentiful pain clinic parking lots. His eyebrows raised in shock and then furrowed in concern as we explained to him all of the information we were gathering during our "stakeouts" of the local pill mills. "Well, first we note the time that we arrive, and we try to vary it so we are there at all different times of the day. Then we count how many cars are in the lot, and then we drive around and write down how many cars are from different counties, and how many cars are from out of state, and then we basically just sit back and chain smoke and watch them go in and come back out with their prescriptions, sometimes five or six people out of the same car!"

"Mmm hmm," he said. "And you ladies have been doing this where?"

"Oh, everywhere," I said.

"All over town," my mom added. "We've probably been to them all by now."

He paused and leaned forward over his desk clasping his hands together. He lowered his head and looked us both in eye. "Ladies, I wouldn't be doing a very good job as the Chief of Knox County if I didn't warn you of the danger of this activity and ask you, beg you, to PLEASE stop staking out the pill mills."

"But..." I tried to interject but was immediately and politely rebuffed.

"Now listen," he said. "I've seen your pretty face on the news more than a time or two. I've heard you on the radio. From what I hear you have quite a following on Facebook, and all of that is wonderful."

"But..." I tried again.

"Listen," he said. "Not everyone is going to be in favor of what you are trying to do. Do you understand me? You're talking about taking away people's drugs. You're talking about trying to cut people off from what they feel like they would die without. They are that desperate. Now, I can't have something happening to you ladies because you're hanging out in a pain clinic parking lot. Let us do the police work. We've got eyes on them."

We both knew that arguing with him was pointless. We were also aware that he had seen a hell of a lot more than we had, and that it would probably behoove us to take his advice, hence our reluctant responses of, "Yes Sir." His warning did strike a chord within me; however, I had no choice but to suffer in silence. I couldn't tell my mother about the messages I had gotten. I couldn't scare her like that.

It began after my first appearance on the six o'clock news. I learned over time to just simply not read the comments on the news website every time they did a story about me, but in the beginning, it was so tempting. For all the people who commented on what a wonderful job I was doing and how grateful they were that FINALLY, at last, someone was taking a stand, there were always those who were against us. Reading ignorant comments about addiction being a weakness rather than a disease would be one thing, but I couldn't bear to read comments like, "Well, there's one less pill head now that he's dead," and, "This is just great. Because her brother was an idiot and killed himself, bitch is going to make the rest of us suffer and take away everyone's meds that actually need it," or the worst, "Stupid junkie got what he deserved . . . natural selection's way of weeding out dumb people that don't deserve to live because of their selfishness." The comments attacking Addison and his character, sometimes celebrating his death, from total strangers were agonizing. They enraged me. My face would become flushed and hot, and red welts would sometimes appear on my neck and chest. My heart raced as my body flooded with adrenaline.

I realized it was best for my own sanity and well-being to never read comments on the news websites. As time went on and I continued to be on the news, on radio talk shows, and in newspaper articles, I didn't have to go to a website to read garbage said about Addison and me. Eventually, the comments started appearing as threatening messages to Addison's Facebook page. Sometimes they came straight to my personal email inbox.

It was the eerie one liners like, "I'd be careful if I were you," or "Watch your back, bitch," that were most disturbing. There were no more than a handful, but "Saw you on the news last night, might want to rethink this crusade you've started if you know what's best for you," is enough to unnerve you, I immediately blocked the Facebook accounts of the people who sent those messages to Addison's page and my personal page, and I moved on. The menacing messages were intimidating for certain, but once they were blocked they left my mind relatively quickly, and at no time did they make me reconsider what I had started.

With the exception of a few of my closest friends, I told no one about the messages, and though my mind immediately returned to them following the Chief's warning, they still seemed nothing more than words out in cyber-space, typed and sent out by some coward hiding behind a keyboard. That is, until someone smashed my bathroom window in the middle of the night. I still somehow convinced myself that whoever had done that was simply trying to scare me, and if that was their goal, their mission was accomplished and over. As frightened as I was, I was certain of two things. First, I had gotten even with them with the shotgun blast through the bathroom door. Second. there was no way I was going to turn back or give up.

<u>the innocent</u>

Depending on where you live, you may have seen commercials about the births of drug addicted babies in reference to the "Opioid Crisis." They are heartbreaking. I can't watch them. They stir within me a dichotomy of emotion. Like most people, I have an incredible sentiment of anger. "How COULD you do that to your baby? HOW COULD YOU?" They are pitiful, they are innocent, and you wonder how the life of an unborn child isn't enough to force someone into sobriety, but that is just how powerful addiction can be. I also feel tremendous compassion for the addict mothers. While many stop at anger, looking at them in disgust, I feel for those mothers. I loved an addict, and through that experience I learned to "love the addict, hate the disease." The chemically dependent brain doesn't make rational decisions. It makes incredibly poor choices and causes the addict to hurt people he or she loves. I can assure you that the average addict feels an incredible sense of guilt and shame for the choices he or she has made, which furthers drug use because the drug numbs the emotional pain. Can you imagine the guilt and shame of giving birth to a baby who is addicted to drugs that *you* ingested? How would you stomach watching your infant writhe in pain from withdrawal?

I feel for those mothers. My heart breaks for them. Gathering statistics on this topic was another difficult task. East Tennessee Children's Hospital (ETCH), fewer than twenty miles from my house, was in the middle of an expansion specifically for opioid addicted newborns. We had more of them to care for than there were beds available. Because ETCH was so well-acquainted with our epidemic, we began gathering information from them and followed up with several of the other major hospitals throughout the state.

Dear _____,

In general, when a particular state is described as being "The Leader," "The Pioneer," or "The Most Knowledgeable," compared to all of the other states in our nation, it elicits a sense of pride, but Tennessee is now "The Pioneer" and "The Leader" of an issue that is NOTHING to be proud of. The rest of the country is now looking to us, the state of Tennessee, and in particular to Knoxville's East Tennessee Children's Hospital with questions about the care of opiate addicted newborns because we are "The Leader" in the United States for Neonatal Abstinence Syndrome (NAS) births. Neonatal Abstinence Syndrome is another devastating repercussion of our prescription drug epidemic.

We not only have thousands addicted to prescription pills, thousands dying from prescription pill overdoses, thousands incarcerated due to prescription pills, but we also now have hundreds, with the numbers soon moving into the thousands, of babies born addicted to prescription pills. In this letter you will be given an accurate and detailed description of the heart-wrenching, painful, and expensive consequences of our rapidly increasing NAS births. Information was provided to me by the staff, doctors, registered nurses, and administrators from our very own Children's Hospital.

Neonatal Abstinence Syndrome occurs when a baby is born addicted to opiates and upon his or her first breath is thrust into the same painful and disturbing withdrawal symptoms that adults endure when attempting to detox from prescription pills. My brother Addison painfully detoxed from opiates several times because he wanted so badly to be free from the addiction of prescription pills. He knew that taking that very first pill, which was not prescribed nor medically needed, was a terrible and life-changing mistake, and one that he wished he had never made. NAS babies never made that mistake. Sadly, these babies are born suffering for their mothers' mistakes and pay dearly for them.

Pregnant women addicted to opiates pass the drugs to their babies through the placenta. One of the reasons that opiate addiction in pregnant women is vastly more devastating and different from other elicit and illegal drugs such as crack cocaine is the mother's inability to stop using the drugs while pregnant. If a pregnant woman were discovered to be addicted to any other drug such as "crack," she would be advised to quit taking it, immediately. Pregnant women addicted to opiates, however, are encouraged to continue the use of prescription pills, or the synthetic counterpart, suboxone, for the duration of their pregnancies under the care and monitoring of doctors because if they immediately stop the abuse of opiates while pregnant, the baby is most likely to die in-utero. This leaves expectant mothers in painful and difficult emotional states, with disheartening immediate futures and fearful long-term futures full of unknowns.

NAS withdrawal symptoms immediately affect the central and autonomic nervous systems as well as the digestive system. Symptoms include but are not limited to:

-Inconsolability
-High-pitched crying
-Hyperactive reflexes
-Tremors
-Seizures

-Sensitivity to light and sound
-Poor feeding or feeding intolerance
-Excessive sucking
-Diarrhea
-Excessive sweating
-Nasal congestion
-Sneezing
-Fever
-Irregular heart rhythm

Because of the severity of these symptoms, NAS babies are immediately placed on a monitored oral dosage of morphine. In many cases morphine is administered in conjunction with up to two other medications, including phenobarbital and clonidine. These babies must be monitored continuously, the environmental stimuli must be kept to a minimum, they have special dietary needs, and they must be swaddled or rocked for extended periods of time.

At East Tennessee Children's Hospital in Knoxville there are 152 beds inside the NICU unit. The unit was recently expanded to accommodate the increasing number of NAS babies born at or transferred to this hospital. There were 135 admissions in 2011, and an additional 160 admissions are projected for 2012. For the six-month period of July-December of 2011, 40% of the NICU population were NAS babies, and in the first quarter of 2012 that number increased to greater than 50%. These numbers are higher than those of any other hospital in the country and continue to grow. Head administrator Sheri Smith, who is also a registered nurse at Children's, stated, "We have yet to reach the apex of this epidemic. Until stricter laws are put into place, and the gross overprescribing of highly addictive opioids is regulated, the numbers of addicted newborns that we care for here will continue to rise."

In 2011, approximately 68% of Children's NAS babies stayed inside the NICU and were able to be weaned using oral administration of morphine, alone, within 24 days; however, 32% of the NAS babies required a weaning time of 60-120+ days and required the oral administration of morphine in conjunction with up to two additional medications. At an average of approximately $10,000 per day, per baby, it is easy to see how expensive it is for our state to care for these infant patients.

In 2011, the cost for caring for NAS babies at Children's Hospital alone was between $48 million and $74 million depending on the duration of the patients' stays in the NICU. At the end of this year, this cost is on track to reach the $53 million - $80 million range. It is also extremely important to note that the "majority" of the NAS patients admitted to Children's Hospital for treatment are on TennCare or have no insurance at all. Furthermore, the following have been identified as definitive and possible "public health issues" regarding NAS babies in our area:

-Elevated healthcare costs to treat a preventable condition
-The majority of NICU beds are being taken by infants whose primary need is NAS withdrawal treatment
-Probable behavioral/learning issues or disabilities in childhood
-Does intrauterine exposure to opioids activate the addictive gene in-utero?
-Does the necessary use of morphine for NAS treatment complicate addictive tendencies?
-Does the permanent and irreversible brain damage which occurs in the opiate-addicted mother reproduce itself in the infant brain?

There are so many unanswered questions as to what challenges these children will face in their futures. Answers that we will not know for many years after much more expense and time is spent with research. What we do know is that these babies are born addicted to drugs that they did not choose to take. We are "The Leaders" in Tennessee, with more of these babies born per year than in any other state in the country. The reason for this is the same reason that we have more people addicted, dying, and incarcerated because of prescription pills. We have one of the most LAX sets of state laws regarding accessibility to prescription drugs in the country, with an epidemic that is the

WORST in our nation and second ONLY to West Virginia. Knoxville's Children's Hospital has been featured twice in recent national news, on CNN and *Nightline*, regarding NAS births. The shows included saddening footage of NAS newborns as well as interviews with the staff, nurses, doctors, and new mothers of NAS babies. Everyone working in legislation has been sent an email link to both of these news stories, and if you did not get the chance to view them, I can assure you they are very difficult to watch. A young, new mother, who was interviewed while holding her screaming child, stated that, ". . . around here it's like a walk in the park to get whatever prescription you need. I have done this to my baby, who deserved so much more. It is my fault for taking these pills, but they were just so easy to get."

The children born addicted to prescription pills are just another heartbreaking result of this epidemic. The cost is great, not only to the newborn babies themselves, but also in actual dollar amounts. It begins with the hospital bills, which alone are tens of millions of dollars, and then extends onto the court costs for custody removal and foster care for these children. You will be receiving more information from the members of A.D.D.I.S.O.N. regarding those matters in the very near future.

I hope that this description of another aspect of our prescription drug epidemic will ignite your support for The Addison Sharp Prescription Regulatory Act for the upcoming legislative session. SO many lives are ending because of prescription pills, like my brother Addison's, which has caused immense heartbreak and pain. What we must consider is that now so many lives are BEGINNING this way as well and will continue to do so unless we do something about it.
Sincerely,
Jessica Sharp Akhrass
(Addison's Sister)

Since I penned this letter, studies have shown that it is possible for addicted mothers of unborn babies to safely, under medical supervision, discontinue opioid use through a step down weaning method while pregnant, without causing the death of the unborn child, but at the time, so many things remain unknown. What we were experiencing was dwarfing the "crack baby" epidemic of the 1980s, and it was becoming obvious that our society is going to be continuously learning about the repercussions of the opioid scourge for the next 30 years at least. While I sent this letter to the legislative body reporting our statistics and findings, the rest of the members of Addison's Facebook page sent their own personal letters on the subject. Many chose to do so anonymously, but they shared their own agonizing experiences of the births of their own NAS babies, those born to loved ones, and several who had chosen to lovingly foster and/or adopt NAS babies. I was inspired at the bravery that it took for so many to share their stories surrounding a topic that carried with it such condemnation, but like me, these thousands were willing because they, too, had had enough.

see you in court

As the summer of 2012 began turning to fall, the members of Addison's Facebook page and I were preparing to send our final letters to our Tennessee legislators. Our final topic not only addressed the Department of Children's Services, but also included a range of other current statistics that we collected from a variety of sources. As with all of our previous correspondence, I sent the first letter introducing the topic and provided all of our data. The Facebook members followed up with personal letters detailing their own experiences. I can't imagine what the legislators' inboxes and mailboxes looked like when it came to the court case letters. The number of people raising the children of family members due to addiction, incarceration, or death from prescription pills was in the thousands from my group alone and well into the upper tens of thousands statewide.

Dear_____,
With this year's election rapidly approaching, I wanted to send you one final letter from A.D.D.I.S.O.N. detailing pertinent statistics, numbers, costs, and facts regarding our prescription pill epidemic in Tennessee. Rather than focusing on one individual topic as in previous correspondence, this letter will cover a broader spectrum of areas that are being negatively impacted by our prescription drug epidemic in our

state. In 2011, there were 26,891 cases of abuse and neglect investigated by Child Protective Services within the Tennessee Department of Children's Services. Of those investigated, close to 10,000 child victims were involved in proven cases of maltreatment. Below is the percentage break down of how prescription pills were involved in over **70%** of these cases statewide.

-DCS cases in which child victims were EXPOSED to prescription pill abuse on a regular and prolonged basis – 29.5%

-DCS cases in which children were victims of NEGLECT due to prescription pill abuse of the parent – 27.2%

-DCS cases in which children were victims of PHYSICAL and MENTAL ABUSE due to prescription pills – 15.1%

Therefore, at 71.8%, over 7,000 children in Tennessee were victims of exposure, abuse, and/or neglect DIRECTLY related to prescription pills last year. Each year this number continues to rise. Not only is this figure emotionally heartbreaking because it involves innocent children, but also the process of investigating, prosecuting, and protecting these children comes at a great financial cost.

Listed below are the procedures and fees that are accumulated in each DCS case involving child victims and prescription pill abuse in the family court system.

-Parents are required to undergo drug and alcohol assessments
-Urine drug analysis ($25 each) and/or hair follicle tests ($300 each) are performed
-DCS court costs (though they do vary) are on average over $1000 PER case
-The state-appointed attorney fees (appointed on the behalf of the child) are between $750-$1000 PER case
-State appointed attorney fees (appointed on behalf of the parents) are an additional $1000 PER case

-Foster care for children removed from their homes costs the state an average of $682 PER child, PER month
-The average length of time a child spends in foster care is twenty months
-Some counties are even ridiculously handing out gas cards to parents so that they have the means to drive to court-appointed routine drug testing

It is difficult to assess "exactly" what this is costing the state per year, but from my research and information provided, we can gather a rough estimate. This estimate has been calculated on the basis of the approximate 7,000 child victims due to prescription pill abuse in 2011 to represent the financial cost for ONE YEAR.

-Urine testing and hair follicle analysis averages $2.2 million per month, for an average total of $27 million per year
-Court costs at an average of $1000 each for 7,000 cases yields $7 million per year
-State appointed attorney fees average between $5 million and $7 million per year
-This number is doubled to $14 million per year if the parents are appointed public defenders
-Of course, not all cases result in the child being placed in foster care if there are other family members willing to take and care for the children; however, if we were to estimate that at least HALF of the 7,000 cases in 2011 resulted in a foster care situation, this financial cost to the state is staggering. For 3,500 children, at $682 per month, this would cost the state $2.3 million per month. Since we do know that each child remains in foster care for approximately 20 months on average, this total yields a cost of $47.7 million.

Though it is impossible to know the exact monetary figure that prescription pill abuse is costing the state of Tennessee regarding DCS cases and child victims, from the estimates listed above, one can gain a general idea. The estimated cost results in over a whopping $100 million dollars in ONE YEAR.

Each letter you have received has provided you with the most current research and analysis of what this epidemic is costing our state. From jail incarcerations, to NAS babies, autopsies, and DCS cases, the epidemic is financially costing us close to ONE BILLION dollars per year, when every facet of this problem is accounted for and added together. One billion dollars is astronomical, and something must be done to alleviate this ever present and continuously growing mega-issue.

The remainder of this letter will include general statistics that are current, accurate, and further prove the necessity of immediate action. The information has been collected from personal research from the Metropolitan Drug Commission, county police chiefs, the Tennessee Department of Mental Health and Substance Abuse Services, and thousands of other Tennessee residents from A.D.D.I.S.O.N., just to name a few.

-Tennessee is now the leading state in the U.S. in pounds of prescription pills (opiates) sold. Approximately 16,000 POUNDS of drugs were dispensed in the state of Tennessee in 2010.
-Prescription opioids ranked the #1 abused drug among individuals receiving state-funded treatment and rehabilitation services.
-Like my brother Addison, 71.2% of people who abuse prescription opiates get the drugs from a friend or relative (this percentage is made possible by the gross overprescribing of prescription opioids from the "pain management" clinics, a.k.a. pill mills, which are running rampant across our state).
-Local pain clinics on average are prescribing between 500-800 pills per month to ONE individual.
-Most opiate addicts spend a minimum of $300 per day each to support their addictions.
-One visit to a pain clinic will cost an individual between $300-400, but when the prescription pills they obtain are sold to their friends and relatives for $30 per pill, the profit margin for dealing can top 2,000%.
-Many addicts trade food stamps for pills and use state-sponsored phones to make drug deals among friends.
-Upon personal surveillance of Knoxville area pain clinics, I observed

thousands of vehicles which had traveled from nearly every other county in the state to our pill mills, including license plates from Georgia, Florida, Kentucky, Alabama, and South Carolina.
-Thousands of cases of prescription pill abuse are being funded through Medicare and TennCare.
-The mass quantity of prescription pills dispensed last year in Tennessee represents:
-51 pills of Hydrocodone for EVERY Tennessean above the age of 12
-22 pills of Xanax for EVERY Tennessean above the age of 12
-21 pills of Oxycodone for EVERY Tennessean above the age of 12
-This means that pain clinics in TENNESSEE prescribed last year, alone, 94 pills for every man, woman, and child from Bristol to Memphis, and this tally does not include other widely abused drugs such as Suboxone, Valium, and Opana.

I hope that this final letter, in conjunction with all of the previous information we have provided for you, will give you a better understanding of just how LARGE this epidemic really is, and that we need immediate action in the state of Tennessee.

As I have stated so many times before, I am not fond of speaking about this issue in terms of figures and budgets. I lost my little brother. He was worth more than any number I have thrown your way. Unfortunately, Addison was one of THOUSANDS of lives we have lost, of people who were all worth more than any dollar amount. I have learned through this process to speak the language of numbers and budgets. I hope that what I have presented is as jaw-dropping to you as it is to me. I hope that by seeing piece by piece every aspect of how we are ALL affected by this epidemic will encourage you to support The Addison Sharp Prescription Regulatory Act in the upcoming legislative session.

I have dedicated every ounce of time, energy, and passion into this cause for the last ten months since I lost my brother. A few days ago was Addison's birthday. He would have been 23 years old. I was 23 years old when I got married. Addison never married. Addison never

graduated from the University of Tennessee. Addison never had a family of his own, nor the chance to grow old alongside me, as my younger brother. He wanted all of those things very badly. One horrible mistake on his part, accompanied by availability of prescription pills as easy to buy as a sandwich, led to his death. Our lives are forever changed, and the hole in our hearts will remain expansive and painful. It is because of that loss, and pain, and devastation, that I dove into this very important cause. What we have experienced in the loss of my brother is so horrific that I will do anything I can to prevent ANYONE else from experiencing it, too. I need your help to make this happen, and I ask for your support in the near future.
Sincerely,
Jessica Sharp Akhrass
(Addison's Sister)

Once all 132 copies of that final letter were mailed, I was forced to quickly switch gears. It was an election year, so no one slept, not that I had been doing much of that anyway. In the few short months prior to November, my mother and I were invited to, and therefore supported and attended, every campaign kickoff, election barbecue, chili supper, political luncheon, bruncheon, and silent auction afternoon tea party for every one of our legislative sponsors who were up for re-election and others from whom we wished to gain support. We worked the voting polls themselves on election day and attended the Crown Plaza Republican Election Party that night.

It was clear that our grassroots campaigning tool had been making quite an impact as I began to socialize with the legislators at every gathering. Even those I had never met seemed to know who I was, if for nothing else than the person who was filling their home mailboxes with plenty of summer reading material. Our tactics were working, they knew who we were, they knew what we stood for, and they knew Addison's name. We could breathe a sigh of relief when all of our sponsors were re-elected, and each independently pledged a vow of reassurance to my mother and me, as well as Addison's Facebook members, that our efforts would not be in vain. As State Representative Jimmy Matlock said, "My God, we were so misinformed about what is going on. We are going to take care of this. I promise you that."

waiting game

We had nothing left to do but wait. We had completed our research, we had sent every letter, and there was nothing left to be done during the fall of 2012 but wait for the upcoming legislative session to begin in January. Still, I was no less busy. I continued to sell A.D.D.I.S.O.N. bracelets across the state and throughout nearly a dozen others. I also continued my speaking engagements with schools, youth groups, and anti-drug events.

While at home, the members of Addison's Facebook page and I continued an uninterrupted flow of information daily. We communicated about different rehab facilities when family members were searching for a way to help a loved one. We posted pictures of the missing, and I updated our prayer request lists sometimes hourly. I still awoke to dozens of messages every morning and remained acutely aware that the death toll continued to rise while we waited. I tried to remain a source of support for those who seemed to have lost all hope while most days still trying to wrap my head around the fact that Addison was gone.

I wrote so many letters and responded to so many messages, that it didn't even seem odd to me when I started receiving requests to write to incarcerated family members of our Facebook group. I agreed. It began as a letter here, a letter there, but before long I was writing to a great number of inmates across the state. My mother even began writing them, too.

They shared their stories of addiction, which were always so similar to Addison's and parallel to each other's. I shared Addison's story and everything that I had been trying to accomplish since his death. They were encouraged and in turn encouraged me. They gave me advice, telling me the lowest of the lows to which they stooped to get another handful of pills. I learned a drug addicts' "tricks of trade," so to speak. They were grateful that someone was trying to help.

I felt so badly for them. Like Addison, they recognized that their choices paired with this disease had done, in some cases, irreparable damage. My mother and I just kept thinking about the loneliness and isolation that addiction can and does create. It wasn't long before we began traveling to different county jails to visit several of the inmates we had been writing.

I'm sure people thought we were insane, and maybe we were. We traveled around to different counties, sometimes traveling for hours to visit a complete stranger in a cold, dark, and dingy jail. We would sit together on a metal bench in the tiny soundproof booths, waiting behind a piece of glass, inches thick and marred with years of smudges and scratches. Different jails allotted the inmates varying amounts of time for visitation. Some allowed twenty minutes, some a half an hour. We always seemed to fill up the time with plenty of conversation, and they always seemed so extraordinarily delighted to see us.

It meant something to them that there were people out there who cared—people who didn't look at them through a thick cloud of judgement but knew that, were it not for this disease they suffered, they would have never committed the crimes that landed them in jail. We understood that they were very, very sick. It meant something to us that we could show them care and compassion and that we brightened several long and seemingly endless days.

Speaking of long and seemingly endless, the year was coming to a close and my family began to dread the rapidly approaching holidays. The first of every holiday or special occasion with an "empty chair" is the hardest. Some like to leave the empty chair in remembrance of the one they've lost. We couldn't stand the empty chair. It had to be removed. We couldn't help but stare at it, and that brought indescribable anguish upon us all. No one could imagine cooking for Thanksgiving that year, so we went out. We tried to tell ourselves it would be better since it was out of the ordinary for us. Something different, no mess, no hassle. I nearly took the server's head off after asking him to remove our one empty chair from the table multiple times and then finally slinging it around to the table behind us myself. The food wasn't great, the service was even worse, and I believe more than half of us ended up with diarrhea that afternoon.

We didn't go to Nassau that year for Christmas. We felt like we needed to be together and couldn't leave my grandparents behind. (Not that we would have been able to go to Nassau and actually be happy.) Without Addison, it just wasn't the same. So once again we decided to do something different, something that wouldn't stir memories of him because it would be new. We packed our bags and headed to Tunica, Mississippi, for a few days of shows and gambling, all of us semi-content and hoping to find anything that was mind-numbing or distracting.

All that can really be said about that first holiday season without him was that we survived. January 2, 2013, was the day that we dreaded most. He had been gone for one year. Three hundred and sixty-five days without Addison. While my body didn't ache from head to toe like it once had, I couldn't say that a year later it felt any easier. Needing to stay occupied, Sam and I, along with my parents, headed to Asheville that day to tour the Biltmore Mansion. It was just a few hours away and was something we had never seen. I can't say that we had a good time, but it adequately diverted our attention. I was just ready to get back to work in Nashville.

Days later I was headed to another meeting in the Legislative Plaza, and a month after that The Addison Sharp Prescription Regulatory Act of 2013 was officially filed on February 17, as House Bill 1264 and Senate Bill 0676. On pins and needles, I checked the Tennessee General Assembly website daily looking for my bill to appear on the calendar, which was another almost two-week wait. Finally, it appeared, and I knew this ride was about to begin. It was a constant adrenaline rush receiving instructions from my legislative sponsors and scrambling to get the word out to the Facebook members before everything would come to a screeching halt again. My life consisted of, "Hurry, hurry, hurry! Now, wait."

I could hardly contain myself when I received word that my bill would be going before the House Criminal Justice Sub-Committee for its first vote on March 12. In preparation for the vote, I looked up all the members of this sub-committee and created an Excel spreadsheet including their names, office phone numbers, and email addresses. I promptly shared it with the thousands of A.D.D.I.S.O.N. Facebook members. Then we paused an eager, anticipatory pause. Three days prior to the vote I unleashed the floodgates on the Legislative Plaza. I had every willing member, which was in the thousands, calling and emailing the House Criminal Justice Sub-Committee members to ask for their support and vote for House Bill 1264. The calls and emails were so overwhelming that one of my legislative sponsors called to ask me if I could make it stop! By the time I made my own call that afternoon, one of the state representative's secretaries answered the phone by saying, "House Bill 1264?" It was fabulous.

I barely slept the night before the first vote. Having the availability to watch the proceedings live on the internet granted me the option of viewing at home, most of the time with my mother, in our pajamas, pacing, chain smoking, and reserved us the right of privacy to not have our shit together should the need to scream, yell, or cry overtake one of us. To make matters worse our bill didn't go before the committee until 4:00 p.m. We had to wait all DAY!

Finally, the time came, and went. Minutes prior to being brought before the sub-committee, I received word that my bill had been rolled to the next week's calendar. POSTPONED. I felt like a deflated balloon. A limp noodle. After the buildup of stress and eager expectancy, we had more waiting to endure. It was something that I was going to have to somehow grow accustomed to and realized early on that God was giving me an important lesson on patience, of which I have very little. My sponsors continued to be supportive, holding my hand through this grueling process that I had poured the entirety of my life into for a full year. Representative Bill Dunn said it best when he told me, "Do NOT get upset unless and until I TELL you to get upset." These people grew to know me so well in such little time.

My emotions didn't change the following week leading up to the first vote. Excitement, anticipation, apprehension, nausea, all were swirling around leading up to . . . another postponement. I didn't think I was going to survive the process. I didn't know how much I could take of this drastic swing of emotion without relief. The waiting was killing me! Not long after the second postponement, a request was made that I travel back to Nashville to attend and give testimony in person before the House Criminal Justice Sub-Committee the following week. Immediately, my mother and I agreed, though between us we very unsure of how we would keep it together throughout the vote. Of course, we had another week of waiting to figure that out.

<u>*testimony*</u>

We felt like we needed reinforcements—moral support. Former court reporter, sister of a local judge, and very "in the know" politically, my godmother was eager to join us in Nashville for my upcoming testimony. Plus she is just fun. To make absolutely sure that we would be 100 percent on time, rather than endure the horrid debacle of being uncharacteristically twenty minutes late to our very first meeting, we headed to Nashville the day before my testimony.

    We positioned ourselves comfortably across the street from the Legislative Plaza at the downtown Hilton. After dinner we retired to our room to go over my speech. We tried to go to sleep before midnight but ended up lying in the dark and talking for hours before finally drifting off into restless and fitful sleep. Morning came quickly, which made us even more thankful that our destination was a short walk away. I'm uncertain at what point I began to tremble, but I do recall being more nervous than I probably had ever been in my life.

    The Plaza was bustling as usual. After making it through the metal detectors at security, we made a beeline to the restroom. As we walked slowly down the wide hallway of the Plaza, looking for the room numbers above each door, I saw a familiar face and couldn't have been more relieved. The

Chief waved to us, and as we hurried toward him I felt a slight calm come over me, however brief. At least we couldn't get lost now. He knew exactly where we were going, and I was not letting him out of my sight. Once inside the room we were seated in the front row, and while we waited for the meeting to commence, the Chief gave me the rundown of the proceedings. It was so nice to know how it would all take place before it happened, though it didn't stop my heart from racing nor my stomach from churning.

State Representative Jeremy Faison was the Chairman of the Committee and began by calling one of my sponsors, Representative Bill Dunn, to the podium, "Representative Dunn, you are recognized."

> Thank you. Mr. Chairman and members of the committee, as a result of the continuing problem of prescription drug abuse and the growing number of lives being lost to overdoses of these drugs, the Public Safety Coalition is supporting the proposed Addison Sharp Prescription Regulatory Act of 2013. Addison Sharp was a resident of Knoxville, Tennessee, whose young life was tragically cut short on New Year's Day 2012 by an overdose of prescription medication. Addison was also on the high school bowling team with my daughter, Elizabeth.
>
> Since this tragedy, his family has worked with legislators, law enforcement, and medical professionals to impact the number of lives being taken by this growing epidemic. Addison's mother, his godmother, and his sister Jessica Akhrass are here today, and I'd like to ask the committee to go into recess to hear from Jessica. She is the one who has put so much time and work into this, and if she could make a few remarks regarding this it would be appreciated.

Representative Faison responded, "Absolutely, without objection we're going into recess." And with the smack of his gavel I knew it was my turn. I had been fidgeting in my seat behind Representative Dunn while he rapidly read his introduction. Everyone always seemed in such a hurry in that building, and I knew that time was always of the essence. I also knew that the statements that I had prepared were a little more than a "few remarks." It didn't help my nerves, but after everything that I had put into being at that hearing, for this moment, I was going to take my time and say everything that I needed to say. This was possibly my one and only shot. I was determined to be heard. I just prayed that my quivering knees didn't buckle.

I approached the podium as Representative Faison helped me introduce myself. "Thank you for being here. Would you tell us your name?"

"Yes, my name is Jessica Sharp Akhrass," I said nervously while trying to adjust the microphone to my face. I requested to hand the clerk 8x10 copies of a photograph of Addison and me so that each member of the committee could see his sweet face as I spoke.

Thank you, members of the committee, for letting me speak today. As Representative Dunn mentioned, one of the lives that was lost to this epidemic was my baby brother Addison. To know Addison was to love him. He was genuine, kind, loving, and sincere, traits that were obvious even when he was a little boy. His sense of humor was beyond compare, and his compassion for others was overwhelming. Addison was also just a normal, everyday kid. Upon graduating from high school in 2008, Addison wanted to get a summer job before starting UT that fall. He was working, for the most part, with other kids his age at an entertainment facility for children, with go-karts, rides and video games. Surprisingly, most of his co-workers were regularly abusing prescription pills, and the assistant manager was dealing pills from that facility. Because of Addison's inexperience, immaturity, and curiosity, Addison took a pill offered to him from co-worker, having no idea what it was, what it would do to him, what it would do to our family, and ultimately what it would end up costing us all.

Addison overdosed on Xanax in January of 2009 and spent almost five months in an all-boys, faith-based rehabilitation center in Arkansas. He did well for several months after he returned, but was then once again, a friend offered him a Roxicet, which was his first experience with opiates.

Addiction is a disease, and what starts out as a fun and euphoric want, quickly changes to a desperate and painful need as the chemistry in an addict's brain rapidly adjusts to the presence of opiates in his system. When this happens, there is an equally severe change in behavior and attitude. It can take a loving and personable, outgoing and caring, sweet young man who would do literally just about anything to help another human being and change him into a lying, manipulative, and detached individual who would now do just about anything to get that next pill.

We watched this happen to my brother. We did everything we could to get him back to us, and he wanted to be back. He hated pills; he hated the mistake that he made that one summer afternoon because he thought it might be fun. He begged for help. He said the pills had eaten his soul and made him do things he would never have considered in the past.

We tried everything to help him and feared every day the thought of jail, or the fact that he could die.

The second half of 2011, for six solid months, Addison was clean. He had been through withdrawals, again, and had gained a lot of weight that he had lost while abusing prescription pills. He looked healthy, he seemed happy, and had changed his major at UT to psychology because he had decided that as a recovering addict, he could help so many people, and that is what he truly wanted. To help. To make an impact, a difference.

We go to the Bahamas at Christmas as a family. That has been our tradition for my entire life. It is our favorite place to go, and we look forward to it every year. That year was no different. We had a wonderful trip, Addison was clean, we were all together, and we were happy. We arrived home New Year's Day of last year. I stood in my driveway when we got home from the airport, and hugged my brother, for what would be the very last time. I told him that I loved him, never knowing that those would be my last words to him on earth.

The next morning my mom went to his room to wake him so that he could go to the vet to pick up his dog. She touched him and he didn't respond. He was already cold. He was dead, and she knew it when she felt his face. Addison had been able to obtain two pills of Opana, a medication that is a combination of OxyContin and morphine used to treat cancer patients. He got them from a friend with a simple phone call, after just arriving back into the country hours earlier, and I know what he was thinking because I knew him so well. He thought, I'll just do this one more time, and then I'll go back to school and everything will be fine.

And it was the last time. As he went to sleep and his respiration depressed, his heart slowed until it stopped, and then he was gone.

Addison was able to obtain any pill that he wanted any time that he wanted because they are so readily available to anyone. Addison never went to a doctor, he never visited a pain clinic, he was never prescribed anything. He never had to go to the doctor because for years he was able to get whatever pain pill he desired from other college students and kids his age, and the list of contacts that he had available to him was extensive, to the tune of about 30 different people. He didn't have to go to a shady part of town or down a dark alley to get them. Pills are available everywhere. They are in schools and neighborhoods in broad daylight and even in our church communities. This availability is a result of the gross overprescribing of addictive and dangerous narcotics from pain clinics throughout our state, and it is affecting literally everyone in one way or another.

Florida was in the same devastating situation a few years earlier than Tennessee. They passed similar legislation to House Bill 1264, which tremendously alleviated their problem. Because of Tennessee's lack of laws and lax regulations, the problem didn't end in Florida. It just moved to Tennessee. Hopefully, you have received over the past year, letters and emails that I have sent to you that not only told Addison's story and the stories of countless others, but also provided you with the most current and accurate data about our epidemic. I am confident of this accuracy because I have gathered all of this data myself, with the help of a Facebook community who has come together as a group for support, to be given a safe place to talk to each other about how this epidemic has negatively impacted, if not ruined, their lives, without having to fear the common judgement of society at large.

There were over 200 newborn babies who came into the world addicted to opiates last year at Knoxville's East Tennessee Children's Hospital alone. Over 200 babies at one hospital. The immediate impact on these babies from the minute they are born is excruciating for them, and it is excruciating to watch. The long-term effects are still unknown, but the list will be long, and it will take us many years to grasp the damage that this has done to the tiniest, most innocent of those impacted.

Our jails across the state are filled past maximum capacity because of prescription drug abuse. Almost everyone incarcerated for charges related to prescription pills has been incarcerated before, and will be again, and again, and again. More than 70 percent of our state's jail populations are filled with inmates who are there because of something related to prescription pills, and I know because I called every single one.

Accidental overdose deaths continue to rise each year that nothing is done to help put a stop to this growing epidemic. Over 3,500 Tennesseans died last year alone from an accidental overdose to prescription pills. According to medical examiners, hospital officials, emergency room doctors, and hospital employees, each year the number grows, and I know because I called about all 3,500. Every single one of those 3,500 accidental deaths was 100 percent preventable. DCS and our court system cannot keep up with all of the cases that are before them that are directly related to prescription abuse. Children are being taken from their parents. Grandparents are given custody when they can be, but the foster care system is exploding because of this.

All of my letters address each aspect that I have listed for you and how it has affected that area in a negative way. I also attached the financial price tag for each area of concern. Passing this legislation will not only save lives, which is of the utmost importance—to preserve the sanctity of life—but passing this bill will also save a lot of dollars. Currently, we are spending each year, on average, 100 million dollars for court cases, 100 million dollars for foster care, 400 million dollars for jail incarcerations, 80 million dollars for the care of NAS newborns, and that's just for East Tennessee Children's Hospital, and six million dollars on autopsies. Notice that this list, unfortunately, does not include state-funded rehabilitation centers, but we can't leave that off of the financial list.

A quick estimation proves that currently we are spending close to one billion dollars per year on prescription drug abuse. What is sad is that not one dollar listed is spent on prevention. Every dime we are spending is to clean up the mess. This legislation will help in prevention. It will help prevent babies being born addicted to pills, which is forcing them to live out the consequences of decisions that they did not make. It will help prevent continuous and repetitive incarcerations, which do absolutely nothing to help the addicted. It will help prevent children being taken from their parents for a period of time or be given to someone else to raise because their parents are unfit due to prescription drug abuse, This bill will help prevent the accidental deaths that are happening every single day. It will help prevent families from being completely devastated from the sudden loss of someone so young, so bright, so capable, like my brother.

As I mentioned before, my Facebook page is named after my brother, with an acronym for Addison: Abolish

Drug Distribution Igniting Support of New-Beginnings. There are thousands of people on this page, and almost every person there has been devastated in some way by this epidemic. So, it isn't just me standing before you because I lost my precious brother. I speak for them. Most have been looking for a voice for some time now, and for whatever reason, they chose me. So, I stand before you today not just as a sister who lost her brother she loved more than life itself, but also as an advocate for the citizens of our great state of Tennessee who have completely had enough of this problem. They have trusted me to be their voice, and I don't take that responsibility lightly. When someone dies from a prescription drug overdose, they write to me. I read the whole sordid and horrible tale, and I read these stories daily because they arrive daily. It is an incredibly hard burden to bear, to get messages of death, destruction, heartbreak, and ruin. I carry it with me. I hurt for them, I cry for them, and I know how they feel. It is a heavy load for me to shoulder in the shadow of my own terrible loss.

This bill will do so many things. It will save an astronomical amount of money. It will give our citizens a ray of hope, when there seems to be no end to tragedy. It will help prevent the preventable accidental overdose deaths, and by bearing my brother's name, The Addison Sharp Prescription Regulatory Act of 2013 will mean that my brother did not die in vain. His compassion for others and his desire to help those affected by addiction will come to fruition, and even in death he will be able to help more people than he could have ever imagined. So, I ask for your support and your vote for this vital piece of legislation. It will indeed save many lives. Thank you.

When I was finished speaking, the chairman thanked me for my testimony, and I assumed that I could return my shaky legs to my seat in the front row of the hearing room But to my surprise, there were members of the committee who wanted to say a few words as well, beginning with State Representative Jeremy Faison. "First of all, I just want you to know that it is an honor to meet you, you and your mother. You are my hero. As legislators we get letters and emails from people daily, and my wife last year said, 'Jeremy, we're getting some letters that I think you need to stop and read.' I stopped and read them, and I was amazed at the vigor, and the research that y'all have done And I thought, *My goodness, I've never seen anyone so passionate about something.* Consequently, I've read every piece of mail that y'all have sent to my house, and I always wanted the chance to get a picture with y'all, and to meet you, and tell you that I support you. In Tennessee, last year we had over 3,000 people lose their lives to an overdose because of this problem, and we have GOT to meet the problem where it's at, and I hope that we can do something about it. I just wanted to publicly say that y'all are my heroes, and if Americans would get as engaged with the things that they are passionate about like you two have, our country would be a lot better off. I wish I had the passion that y'all have. It's amazing, and God bless y'all. Thank you so much for coming up here and sharing your passion with us. It's infectious, and it's a good, noble, just cause. Thank you."

To say that it was humbling for someone to call me his hero is an understatement. I was just grateful that they hadn't cut me off citing "time constraints." Within minutes of my testimony the committee was ready to vote. They wasted no time, and before I really knew what was happening the gavel smacked again and it was over. A unanimous pass! Our first victory! Though we shouldn't have been surprised at another schedule change, we were caught off guard while taking celebratory photographs in the hallway when we learned that our bill was also up for a vote on the senate side that same day. I was ushered down the hallway to a senate hearing room, and I was asked, "Will it be a problem to keep your testimony to a three-minute time slot?"

Eyes wide, I stared straight ahead and lied. "Nope! Not a problem at all!" The speech that I had prepared and had just presented to the House committee was nearly fifteen minutes long. Now I had five minutes to cut out twelve minutes of what I needed to say to convince these people to vote in our favor.

I scrambled, marking through line after line furiously with a pink highlighter. Having no time to read over what I had done; all I could do was pray that what I said made sense. My contribution was over in a flash and while waiting for all of the other speakers, I had to smile when I saw Senator Ken Yager presenting our bill to the Senate Health and Welfare Committee wearing his A.D.D.I.S.O.N. bracelet. The senate hearing took twice as long as the House Committee. There were many more questions asked by voting legislators; a doctor in particular who clearly had concerns about our goals and would inevitably slow us down at every subsequent vote. He ultimately voted for our bill every time, and we determined quickly that he just really, really, really enjoyed the sound of his own voice.

The senate vote ended with the same glorious outcome as it had in the House. A unanimous passage onto the next set of committees and votes. *Not bad to have so much success all before lunch*, I thought. Many of our Facebook page members had watched the proceedings on the internet, and they were exploding with excitement. We could barely contain ourselves and headed to the Opryland Hotel for a celebratory lunch before heading home to Knoxville. Never before, and never since, have I been on such an emotional rollercoaster. The lows were so low, but the highs I quickly learned were quite high, and we had God to thank for it all.

casting votes

I assumed that once I had completed giving my testimony in Nashville before the Criminal Justice Sub Committee that I would be able to pull myself together and get my nerves under control. I was so wrong. This did not happen, not even a little bit. Over the next three weeks, as our bill continued on through committee after committee; Criminal Justice Full, House Health Sub, Senate Finance, Government Operations, and on and on and on. I existed in a continuous state of sleep deprived panic.

The last-minute schedule changes continued and were excruciating. As our Facebook machine of making calls to legislators' offices to ask for votes would be in full swing, I'd be anxiously pacing the floor waiting for the next committee vote, only for the rug to be pulled out from under me as they slammed on the proverbial brakes with another postponement or schedule change. Conversely, there were moments I would have finally reached relaxation or would be completely passed out from emotional exhaustion to be awoken by the startling ring of the phone to hear, "Our bill will be up for the next vote in ten minutes!"

"Ten minutes? We haven't had time to call anyone! How could it be up in ten minutes? It wasn't supposed to happen until tomorrow!"

I watched every painstaking minute of senate and house committee votes on the internet. Sometimes chain smoking with my mother at her house, sometimes walking in circles in my pajamas at my house, and a time or two bent over the toilet with the laptop on the floor next to me while Sandy held my hair and a wet wash cloth to my neck as I puked, but God is so good. Despite my inability to get a grip on myself, He was so faithful. Our bill went through umpteen sub and full committees in both the house and senate, and not only continued to pass each and every time, but also passed unanimously each and every time. Newspaper articles were written about it: "Bill restricting sale of prescription pills sails through committees." We were on the news: "Prescription pill restriction measure memorializes 22-year-old, tonight at six." Our Facebook page continued to grow as it was shared thousands upon thousands of times.

The last stop on our journey finally arrived on April 18, 2013. Our bill had unanimously passed through every committee until it was time to be presented on the House and senate floor for the final votes. The only things that stood in the way of Governor Haslam's signature turning our bill into a law were two conclusive votes. We had the option of traveling to Nashville to be present for the proceedings, but ultimately decided it best to watch from home. I arrived at my parents' house that afternoon, on what was the 32nd legislative day of the 108th Tennessee General Assembly, laptop in hand, prepared for anything.

The Lieutenant Governor, Ron Ramsey, began with a few smacks of the gavel as he called for the senate to come to order, the members to be invited in, and the doors to be closed. The members and guests were then led in the Pledge of Allegiance to the Tennessee and American flags before the role was called, showing 31 members present. Senator Yager was introduced, and there were several minutes of amendments adopted and explained in rapid fashion as my mother and I sat staring, hearts pounding, trying to keep up.

Senator Yager was then recognized to introduce our bill, and I'm not sure that we took a breath until he finished.

> *Thank you, Mr. Speaker, I appreciate the opportunity to speak to this bill. Of course, this bill has many moving parts but essentially what we are doing in summary, as a collaborative effort between citizens, legislators, and law enforcement, as well as medical professionals across the state, we're trying to tighten up the provisions and essentially make it harder to keep the supply of prescription pain pills out of the hands of persons who shouldn't have them. Mr. Speaker, there are several things that this bill does, and I am happy to take you through the principal ones and entertain any questions that you may have.*
>
> *Amongst the principal provisions of the bill, it directs the Commissioner of Health to develop a standard of care on prescribing of abused and diverted prescription medications, and to provide this to the licensing board to oversee the professionals, with the requirement that they be, in turn, provided to the professionals who would prescribe these medications. It requires additional continuing education on the subject of prescribing opioids, and as Senator McNally has indicated in his amendment, it does limit the dispensing of opioids to a limit of a 30-day supply at a time.*
>
> *In addition, it requires folks who prescribe and dispense from their offices to report to the Controlled Substance Monitoring Database, which had not been done in the previous law, and it requires people who use pain*

management clinics to have a current and valid government issued identification card, so that will give us a better way to identify and track doctor shoppers. It limits the medical director at pain management clinics to four clinics. We don't think a medical director really has time to handle more than four clinics at one time, and it puts an end to the cash business at these clinics, by limiting payments to checks or credit cards except for your copays or your deductibles. It also ramps up the fines on violators of the regulations that govern our pill mills, from $1,000 a day to up to $5,000 a day.

I've taken us through it quickly because I know that we have a lot to do today, but as I said, what we are trying to do is stem the tide of prescription pills flooding this state. Everyone in this room probably has a friend or perhaps a family member who has been affected by the abuse of prescription drugs, and it has reached epidemic levels in our state, and we have worked together for over a year. My co-sponsor Senator Massey and I met with Senator McNally over a year ago to begin working on this bill because of this gentleman right here. You should all have a black and white photo of this guy; this is Addison Sharp.

My mother burst into tears, and I dropped to my knees as Senator Yager held up an 8x10 photo of Addison and me. It was the last photograph taken of us together, just two nights before his death, and it was a total shock to us both when he held it up for the gallery to see.

Addison Sharp was in the prime of life, in his early twenties, and he died from an overdose of prescription pain medication. He had the world on a string, and everything was in front of him, but unfortunately and tragically, he lost his life, and if the statistics are true, while we are talking about this bill right now somebody's going to die in Tennessee from an overdose of prescription drugs. I would like to think that this bill would provide the ultimate answer to every problem we have. I hope it does, but the problem has become so severe that we may have to come back. Mr. Speaker, I appreciate your letting me have a little time to discuss this because it is an important bill, and I would be happy to take any questions or yield to my co-sponsors because I'm sure that they are very passionate about it as well.

Immediately, Senator Haile was recognized.

Mr. Speaker, I rise in full support of this bill, and first off, I'd like to declare Rule 13, and with the sponsors' approval I'd like to be added as a co-sponsor to this bill. This is a serious problem in Tennessee, and we are all fully aware of that, but I want to give a little warning to our members that you can expect some phone calls because this will limit to a 30-day supply from a 120-day supply. I fully support that reduction. I don't necessarily like having a lock on my door, but I do that because of necessity. In fact, I've locked myself out a time or two, and so you may find that you have some inconvenience from this, also, but the benefit is well worth the sacrifice that might take place, so I strongly support this bill. Thank you, Mr. Speaker.

Senator Massey followed.

Thank you, Mr. Speaker. A year ago, the day before session started, I received a phone call from Addison's sister Jessica, and that started the journey that Senator McNally, Senator Yager, I, the police chiefs, and others, began with Jessica's help. We have traveled to get this bill to where it is today. As Senator Yager said, there have been many organizations that we have worked with, including the Tennessee Medical Association and a lot of other folks, to craft and to make sure that we had this bill where we needed it to be. This bill WILL SAVE LIVES, and it is an important piece of legislation. As our Juvenile Court Judge in Knox County says, "Virtually every child that is taken out of a house from families, is [removed] because of a prescription drug problem." Our jails are crowded with people from prescription drug problems. This bill will make a difference, and I appreciate the sponsors' efforts, and everybody else that worked on this, and I would appreciate everybody's support of this bill. Thank you.

Several other members stood to invoke Rule 13, which we found out was a request to become a co-sponsor on the bill. Of course, no senate hearing would be complete without our doctor friend senator who needed a few minutes to ask questions and to give his two cents on what his thoughts were, being a physician and all. Once he had been provided a sufficient amount of time to hear the sweet sound of his own voice, he, too, requested to be a co-sponsor on our bill before returning to his seat.

The Speaker then asked if there were any further questions or discussions on Senate Bill 0676, and when none were raised he rang the bell, which to me always sounded like the starting gate at a horse race. As the members began to vote, we watched as the electronic board with everyone's name listed in white letters all began to change to green with every "Aye" vote that came in. "Has every member voted?" the speaker asked. "Mr. Clerk, take the vote!" he yelled.

"Ayes, 31. No Nays."

"Senate Bill 0676: Having received Constitutional Majority, I hereby declare it passed!"

And just like that, it was done. We cried and just stared at each other in disbelief. We knew that we had to repeat the same process on the House side, but the relief that came with knowing all voting in the senate was complete was engulfing. Becky Massey called my phone to congratulate me as my mother called everyone we knew, beginning with my dad, who was still at work.

I had been told that the full House vote would happen the following day but was not surprised when I began receiving calls and texts to let me know that Representative Dunn had decided to move forward with presenting our bill on the House floor that evening. We barely had time to catch our breath from the senate proceedings before it started all over again in the House. I did have time at least to alert everyone on Facebook so that some, however few, may have a chance to call or email the House members to ask for their votes.

My dad made it home in time to join my mother and me in watching the conclusion of the last sixteen months of work. Representative Dunn began introducing our bill by talking about how Addison had gone to Catholic High School and was on the bowling team with his daughter Elizabeth. He mentioned my mother and me and thanked us for all of our work before diving into the specifics of the bill, much like

Senator Yager had done prior. I paced the floor as we listened. My heart pounded as I grappled with the idea that this was actually IT. In moments, we could be done. After all of my time, my blood, sweat, and tears, we were so close to finally being finished.

I thought of Addison, unsure of how much the Lord allows people to know, see, or understand from Heaven, but I just kept thinking of how happy he would be at all that we had done. All he wanted for his future was to help others who were in combat with the disease that he fought. If we were successful, the number of people we would be helping was far beyond anything that he could have ever imagined. My breath caught in my throat as the bell rang, indicating the final vote on the House floor. Watching the names on the monitor turn green in rapid succession, I was unable to close my mouth. It felt like it had all happened so fast, but simultaneously time seemed to slow down when the final vote was called and it took me a moment to realize that the tally was 93 – 0 in our favor.

We were done. Our bill passed unanimously on the full House floor. It was over, and we had done it. We couldn't believe it. I couldn't decipher what emotion to have first. Joy, elation, relief, triumph, alleviation—they all came at once. There was also sorrow. I had just completed almost a year and a half of the most grueling work I had ever done, all to help prevent others from having to live through the tragedy that we had been forced to endure, and all in Addison's name, and I was a success. We were a success. But Addison was still gone. There was still the realization that I would continue to wake every morning for the rest of my life feeling his absence. Even with the joy of what God had just allowed us to accomplish, there would still be no more memories made with my brother. I couldn't call and tell him how excited we were. Deep inside there was still an emptiness that only he could fill.

Facebook erupted with excitement. Addison's Facebook page, as well as my own, exploded with likes, shares, comments, and more shares. Part of me felt like we had won the lottery, or the grand prize on a game show, and everyone who had participated and journeyed with us throughout the last sixteen months celebrated right alongside us. Before I left their house to come home and tell Sam about everything that had happened, my mother kissed my face. She had tears streaming down her own as she looked up at me from her tiny, 5' 2" stature. "I have never been more proud of you," she said.

john hancock

The month of May 2013 was a blur. Following our success, I went on a local media tour discussing our new state law. I had radio and television invitations for what seemed like weeks. In the midst of it all, my morning ritual of waking to read Facebook messages did not end. The devastation in the lives of those around me had not ceased simply because we had come to the close of our legislative journey. After much prayer and consideration, and several conversations with close family and friends, I decided to step away from Facebook for a while. It was more like those around me convinced me, however reluctant I was, that I needed a break.

    Walking away from this large group of people that I had become so attached to was difficult. I felt so incredibly guilty, though I knew that my heart would never heal as long as I continued to grieve on a daily basis with these strangers that I had grown to love. I wrote a long post thanking them all for their help, for their prayers and support, and was, as usual, candidly honest about how badly I felt for walking away from them. Fortunately, they were so kind in their responses and graciously encouraged me to finally take some time for myself, which I hesitantly took.

From then on, I limited my Facebook time with them to only posting updates about when our bill would finally be signed into law.

God sent me an angel, Sandy Jones, on June 4, 2012, just months after Addison died. She showed up on my front porch just to let me know, however odd that it seemed, that God had sent her to be an encouragement to me and that I would be a success in this mission. She then walked beside me and prayed me through the entire experience. So, it seemed no coincidence that The Addison Sharp Prescription Regulatory Act of 2013 was scheduled to be signed into law by our Governor in Nashville on June 4, 2013, one year to the day that Sandy showed up outside my door.

We took two cars to Nashville that morning. My parents and my godmother were in the smoking car, while Sam and I, along with Sandy, led the way in the non-smoking car. Thankfully the interstate was traffic-free all the way into Nashville. I had hoped that the bill signing would be open to the public, and even more convenient, that it would be held in Knoxville. I knew that so many of our Facebook members would have liked to attend, but it was decided that our bill would be signed along with about 30 others that day in a closed ceremony in Nashville.

We met Becky Massey outside a large auditorium in the Legislative Plaza just after twelve o'clock noon. My family and I sat in the front and watched the spacious room as row after row of seats began to fill with more and more people. We spoke very little as we all sat in quiet reflection of the whirlwind we had survived over the last year and a half. Part of me still couldn't believe that we had made it this far and that this was actually happening.

On the stage in front of us was a long banquet table draped in a black tablecloth, behind which stood the

American and Tennessee Flags. I was startled when someone called out, "Addison Sharp! The Addison Sharp Prescription Regulatory Act!" We all stood and made our way to the side of the stage. The intern at the bottom of the stairs explained to us what we were supposed to do upon her cue that Governor Haslam was ready for us.

Within minutes we filed up the staircase and onto the stage. We were accompanied by Senators Becky Massey and Randy McNally, as well as Representatives Bill Dunn and Ryan Haynes. I got to stand in the middle of everyone, directly over Governor Haslam's shoulder. I couldn't help but smile and whisper, "Thank you, Lord," as I watched him sign his John Hancock onto the documents in front of him with a personalized "Governor Bill Haslam" black Sharpie marker that I was allowed to keep. A photographer standing in front of the stage snapped photos of us during and after the signing. When we were finished, the Governor turned to face me, stuck out his hand to shake mine, and said, "Well done on all your tireless work. Congratulations."

I did feel satisfied as we descended the stairs on the opposite side of the stage, but my thoughts were never far from Addison and his absence. Yes, we had done it. Yes, the new Tennessee law had been named after him. Yes, it would save countless lives. But, but NO, I would still never see his face again on this side of Heaven and the ache that comes with that knowledge was and is unbearable. I was still trying to come to terms with the fact that no matter what I did or how hard I worked, nothing was going to bring him back, and that was difficult to process for quite a long time.

We were exhausted, both emotionally and mentally. I had my picture taken on the steps of the Legislative Plaza before we left, but there was no celebratory lunch to follow, we were all just ready to make the drive back home to rest. I had hoped that with the excitement that we had all felt with the bill's passage, that it would be a feeling that we could all ride on for a little while. I hoped it would make us all happy for a change and give us a reason to smile. I rode on it for a little longer than everyone else. My mother, the least. She returned to her bed and to her sadness within a week.

I didn't quite know what to do with myself when it was all over. I knew that I didn't want depression to overwhelm me again, and so I aimed to stay active. I worked out, I rode my horse, I tried to act normal. Everyone around me had returned to life as usual so quickly, and I strove to keep up. I began having thoughts about writing a book about this whole experience and incredible journey that God had just led me on, but I'd never written a book before. *Wasn't it a little narcissistic? Who would care? Did I write well enough to actually author a book?* With all of the questions and doubts I had, praying about it seemed like the only thing that I could do. So, as I sat on my front porch in my usual spot, that's just what I did.

"Well, should I write this book or not?" I asked aloud. "Seems kind of self-indulgent, maybe?" But the only response the Lord kept sending me was a reminder of what Sandy had been telling me, "God's not done with you yet. There is something even bigger." I didn't know what she meant at the time, and she would admit that she didn't really know either, but she was certain that the bill being passed was not the end of my story. I began to feel more and more confident that the Lord was confirming my questions and pushing me to write, but just when I thought my conversation with God was complete, and that He had given me my newest set of directions, I heard, "Just one more thing; write the book, but also have a baby."

I laughed. "I don't want a baby. I never wanted a baby. We decided we weren't ever going to have a baby, and that's the end of that." I got up from my praying perch and marched myself to my bedroom, where I knew that if I told Sam what I had just prayed about and what I felt the response was, he would affirm that we don't want a baby, we never wanted a baby, we decided we weren't ever going to have a baby, and that would be the end of that. Boy oh boy was I in for a shock. I stated, "Well, I'm definitely supposed to write the book, but you won't believe this. I'm also pretty sure we are supposed have a baby. I have NO idea where THAT came from," I laughed.

Sam looked at me with a completely straight face and responded, "Okay!"

I froze. "I'm sorry, am I in the *Twilight Zone* or something? Okay, what?"

His next response would change the course of our lives forever. "Okay, let's have a baby."

life goes on

For me, having a baby would not be as easy as it is for most. I knew this going into it, and I think that might have contributed to my early decision to never have one. Basically, I didn't think that I could be pregnant. I had female problems since the very late start of my first period at nearly sixteen years old, and that was my main problem—no periods. No period, no ovulation, therefore no baby *But God told me to do this, right? So, He would fix it, right?*. At least that's how I thought it would go. How it went led us on another exhaustive four-year journey with twists and turns, surprises, joys, sorrows, hope, and pain, and a story that could be quite literally, a whole other book.

Up until I was 30 years old, my life had been easy, too easy, I suppose. I never knew real sorrow. Soul-searing pain had never touched my life. When I was 32 years old it all changed. Addison was gone, I knew my life would never be the same, and I often wondered when or if I would ever learn to live again.

My mother had the same experience, though in the aftermath, her fight was just gone. Three years went by, and in the middle of our baby journey when I was 35 years old and had somehow survived losing my beloved brother, life abruptly changed again.

Of course, it was January. The dreaded month during which we lost Addison. We all hated January. Just six weeks prior, I suffered my second miscarriage in a row. I was feeling better and somewhat hopeful.

That January night, I called my mother, or maybe she called me, I can't remember. What I do remember is the time. It was eight o'clock. She was getting ready to watch the Miss Universe pageant, a time-honored tradition for us Southern women. I don't remember much of what we said, and I don't clearly recall us saying "I love you" before we hung up, but I'm sure that we did because we always did.

I knew something was wrong when my phone rang at eleven o'clock that same night. I never expected as the devastating sound of my father's panicked and uncontrollable voice stammering, "She's not breathing! She's not breathing!"

"Who?!" I screamed.

"Your mother!" I went into shock, I guess. I don't remember the ride to the hospital. I remember being led back to Room One, AGAIN. Damn that room. I know that I have never seen my father more frightened, and I know that I was overwhelmed with confusion in trying to understand how all of this had occurred from a simple asthma attack.

My mother had had asthma since she was eighteen. She controlled it with medication and her inhaler, which she was never without. Throughout my lifetime my dad had to take her to the emergency room to have a breathing treatment during particularly bad attacks, but those times were rare. I watched my mother have a thousand asthma attacks. She never seemed afraid. It was just something that she dealt with, and that we all became accustomed to. Sometimes she would have one of us hit on her back to loosen up her contracted muscles, and there were pressure points in her shoulders that would relieve the tension. After over 40 years of marriage, my dad knew exactly where they were.

It never occurred to me during any of these asthma attacks that we had all witnessed dozens upon dozens of times, that they could kill her. When the nurse motioned for us to enter the "family" room, my father and I knew what was getting ready to happen, though we had opposite responses. While I began protesting, "No, No, No, I'm not going in there, this can't be happening."

He hung his head saying, "Yep, here we go, we have to go in that room again. My God." We all stared in disbelief as the doctor entered and in an unbelievably uncaring fashion explained to us that they had revived my mother from cardiac arrest, but that ". . . there's no way she's surviving this. She's not going to live."

Thanks asshole.

I had no idea she was having a "bad breathing day" as she always called them. I had just spoken to her at eight o'clock. She didn't mention it. Everything had come on so quickly. When her inhaler didn't help, and all of dad's efforts to pat, hit, and squeeze her back weren't working she said, "You're gonna have to take me." By the time my dad got his jeans on and emerged from their closet, he found her lying on the floor, having fallen out of a chair, not breathing, and in complete cardiac arrest. Once the paramedics got her heart beating again, her brain had been without oxygen for more than 30 minutes. She continued to code six more times.

So, there she lay, in Room One, on life support, and here we were again. She had given up. I just kept desperately asking my dad, "What are we going to do?"

The only reply that I got was a pitiful, "I don't know."

Over the next couple of days while waiting for the tests to

confirm brain death, everyone that had ever known and loved my mom came to say "goodbye" to her as she lay in ICU. She was so loved. The waiting room was packed. I lay in bed with her and talked. I told her I loved her a thousand times and told her to tell Addison how much I loved and missed him. We gave permission to donate her organs, which meant they had to leave her hooked up to all of the machines. I was so grateful for that. I doubt I could have handled watching them turn everything off and hearing all of the beeping subside and the silence that would have followed.

She had prayed to go home. She had begged God to heal her heart. She had longed for Addison for three years and had expressed to everyone that no matter how hard she prayed she just could not rejoin the living. It just proves that your heart can be broken but it keeps beating just the same. My mother had walked around with a broken heart for three years, and I knew that finally she was no longer hurting. That said, being genuinely happy for her has been extremely difficult. I miss her so badly.

There is nothing truer than this quote by Jamie Anderson, I know because I live it daily. "Grief, I've learned, is really just love. It's all the love you want to give, but cannot. All that unspent love gathers up in the corners of your eyes, the lump in your throat, and in that hollow part of your chest. Grief is just love with no place to go."

I want to call my mother every day. I want her to be by my side, watching the world being experienced for the very first time through my daughter's blue eyes. Yes, you read that right. My daughter was born on December 30, 2016, to two of the most excited parents God has ever created.

I hadn't posted anything in so long but was excited to share the news of her birth with the members of Addison's Facebook page on the day that we were to bring her home from the hospital.

January 2, 2017

Five years ago today, my life was forever changed. I awoke that morning on January 2nd to find that a piece of my heart had suddenly gone with the unexpected passing of my precious brother, Addison. No one and nothing could help ease that pain, and as the saying goes, I did have to "learn to live with it."

It was the kind of pain that eventually led to the sudden death of my mother as well, three years after Addison, when an asthma attack that I had witnessed her have on thousands of occasions claimed her life. Her heart and her little body couldn't take anymore, and she wanted to go Home. There were many days when I couldn't blame her. So much heartbreak, and such tremendous loss, was only magnified by also losing three precious babies in the last four years due to miscarriage. The last five years of my life, beginning that January 2, have been an uphill, seemingly never-ending battle.

But I serve an awesome, and amazing God. He sent the right people to walk by my side through the fire. They are all very aware of who they are, and I love each and every one of them. Four days ago, he sent me someone who will never replace nor heal the space left from losing Addison, but has grown my heart even larger, and has redeemed in a way that ONLY Christ can, the capacity for me to love beyond my wildest dreams.

Miss Riley-Addison Hanna Akhrass was born at 4:12 p.m. last Friday, weighing 7 pounds, 1 ounce, and measuring 19.25 inches long. She is, of course, the most beautiful thing I have ever seen. She looks very much like her daddy, and as an extra precious gift from the Lord, she has her Uncle Addison's beautiful eyelashes and my mother's blue eyes. Addison and my mother would have adored her, and I will do my very best throughout her life to teach her about who her uncle and grandmother were.

So many of you on Addison's page hold such a special place in my heart and were part of the many who walked by my side through the fire, helping pass life-saving legislation carrying my brother's name and encouraging me every step of the way. Now his law is not the only thing that carries his name, and I know that his niece will wear it proudly.

Much Love,
Jessica

dear family

Dear Family,
This letter is to the parents, to the siblings, to the children, or to any other family member who has a loved one suffering from the disease of addiction, and it is a DISEASE. For those who disagree, I implore you to do some quiet research on the subject, speak to a physician, and listen to the facts. Addiction is a disease that has a high genetic component, resistant to treatment, and subject to relapse. Addiction is a disease that destroys virtually everything in its path.

Though it is passed down for generations in many families, no one is immune. Rich, poor, black, white, brown, educated, uneducated, addiction has no boundaries. The fact that it has now hit your home may come as a complete shock to you, or maybe not. Now that it has, it doesn't really matter, though. The only question now is, what the hell are you supposed to do? We all do the best we can with the information that we have at the time. When my brother Addison became an addict, there were no stories in the news about "The Opioid Crisis" or the nation's "Drug Epidemic." It was largely an unspoken topic that had not yet reached newsworthy attention, so we did the best we could.

I am not a physician, or an addiction specialist, or a counselor, but I am a sister who walked along-side her very sick brother for four years. I lived it. I don't have all the answers, but possibly there is someone who is searching, desperately seeking direction down a dark and unknown path. Perhaps it's you. All I can offer is perspective, and a few words of encouragement to let you know that, though loving an addict can sometimes feel like a very lonely, isolating world, you are not alone.

My first and foremost words of advice would be to pray. Pray hard, pray often, pray expectantly, but also pray knowing that whatever the outcome, God is not wrong. I spent a lot of time after Addison died being so very angry at God. Angry for not healing him, angry for taking him away from me. It wasn't until much later that He revealed to me that He did in fact answer my prayers. My prayers for healing, my prayers for Addison to be "normal." He took him home, and at this very moment, because Addison was a believer in Christ, he IS healed; he is, in fact, better than he has ever been. So, my prayers were answered, just not in the way I expected or desired. His ways are not our ways, and sometimes that is a difficult concept for us. If you do not have a relationship with Jesus Christ, I encourage you to start one. It's as simple as calling out to Him. He is always there, and He wants a relationship with you.

Second, accept the fact that you cannot help an addict who does not want to be helped. Also accept the fact that even if the addict does want to be helped, you cannot do it for him or her. No matter how much love, no matter how many tears, no matter how much you beg, no matter how much the addict loses or how many of his friends die, addiction is still a disease with a 40 to 60 percent relapse rate, and the outcome of sobriety is ultimately up to the addict and God. Addison denied his situation for quite some time, but he finally came to the point of not only freely admitting it but also begging for help. He wanted nothing more than to be better, but studies have shown that the longer an addict has been clean, the more dangerous and subject to overdose a relapse becomes, which is exactly how we lost him.

Don't love an addict to death. Looking back, I can see and admit how much my family and I enabled Addison. We didn't know any better and didn't know what else to do. While those suffering from addiction do need help from those who love them, don't love them so much that it enables addictive behavior. Don't continue to make excuses, make life too easy, or continue to let them live with the knowledge that because you are family that they will always, always, always, have a soft place to fall. "Tough love" is difficult because there is a fine line and every person is different. How tough is too tough? Or how do you know if it's enough? Those are questions every family must answer for themselves.

Please don't isolate yourself because you are embarrassed. This is one of the number one stigmas that I tried to break on Addison's Facebook page. So many people fighting this life or death battle do so behind closed doors for fear of judgment. They silently scream on the inside for someone to talk to and someone to listen. When Addison was struggling, no one in our community talked about it openly. After he died, and I began not only talking about it, but also publicly talking about it without shame, many looked at me like I was from another planet, but those who were in the thick of their own silent struggles ran to me and clung to each other because we were safe. Not everyone will be safe, but don't allow that fear to keep you silent. More people are affected by this disease than you know. Put yourself out there. Be the brave one willing to be open and honest without being ashamed. You will find you have more friends than you realize.

Pay it forward with prevention. One of the saddest realizations I made while getting our law passed was the astronomical amount of money our state and the nation were spending on the drug epidemic and how very little of it is for prevention. You may be saying, "Well I already have an addicted loved one I am trying to help, so prevention won't do us very much good at this point." It may not help the addict, but it can help everyone else in your family, especially children. In my opinion and from my experience, you cannot start too early to educate your children about the dangers of drug abuse. They need to be taught early and often, and in particular when it comes to prescription drugs. Just because medication comes with a prescription and from a doctor does not mean that it is safe or non-addictive.

Never give up hope. Take a deep breath, and take one day at a time, which I know is such a cliché because it's not as if three or four days at a time is an option. What I mean by that is to just keep breathing and continue to take care of yourself every single day. You will be no good for your loved one if you stop caring for yourself. Wake up each morning knowing that it is a new day, and that God is ABLE. People are not exaggerating when they call the disease of addiction a *demon* because it is. Well ,who better to fight demons than God, Himself, so please do not give up hope that your prayers will be answered.

And lastly, if you are called, make a difference. It may not be for your entire state or writing and passing a law like it was for me. It may be about speaking up and speaking out in your child's school, in your church community, or around your neighborhood. Maybe your calling is bigger than mine. Maybe your journey will lead you to Washington, D.C., to pass laws for the entire country. Maybe your calling is to further educate our nation about the epidemic that kills hundreds of thousands of people each year. Just as my angel, Sandy, showed up to encourage me, let me now encourage you.

You may think, "Well, I'm just a mom, or just a dad, and I don't know how to go about doing any of that." Take it from "just a sister" with absolutely no government experience. I had no idea what I was doing! But look at all I was able to accomplish. So please, don't let your lack of knowledge or inexperience stop you because if you are called, and you have God on your side, there is NOTHING that will stop you from making a difference.

Before I say goodbye, please remember that you are not alone. There is someone who prays for you. There is someone who understands your desperation and your hurt. There is someone who knows the worries that go through your mind when you are trying to fall asleep at night and understands the dismal thoughts arrive just moments after you wake. The road you are on is treacherous. It is long, and it is hard, and the answers are never easy.

People have told me that they don't understand how I remain so strong. First of all, I don't feel strong most of the time, but my answer to them and encouragement to you is, "You don't know how strong you are until you have no other choice." Stay strong, don't give up hope, rely upon the Lord, and know that you are not alone.
Sincerely,
Addison's Sister

The Addison Sharp Prescription Regulatory Act of 2013 went into effect in October of that year and was the most extensive anti-drug legislation passed in Tennessee state history.

From the first quarter of 2013 to the last quarter of 2017: Prescriptions for opioids in Tennessee decreased from 2 million to 1.6 million.

Prescriptions for Benzodiazepines in Tennessee decreased by approximately 100,000 prescriptions.

Prescriptions for Buprenorphine (Subutex) for medication-assisted treatment increased in Tennessee by approximately 100,000 prescriptions.

The number of pain clinics in the state of Tennessee dropped from it's all time high of 333 down to 158.

Drug overdose deaths in the state of Tennessee unfortunately continue to steadily rise due to the increase in the abuse of street heroin followed by the massive influx of fentanyl.

Jessica and her husband Sam welcomed another blessing of total surprise on Valentine's Day of 2019. A son, Jameson Jeffery, was born. He, too, has Addison's eyelashes and his grandmother's blue eyes.

www.ingramcontent.com/pod-product-compliance
Lightning Source LLC
Chambersburg PA
CBHW020523080526
44583CB00013B/721